BRIDGES TO UNDERSTANDING

MARGARET FRAKES

Bridges to Understanding

The "Academy Movement" in
Europe and North America

MUHLENBERG PRESS PHILADELPHIA

Library of Congress Catalog Number 60-13906

Printed in U.S.A. UB 873

TO PAUL HUTCHINSON

1890–1956

FOREWORD

This little book aspires to be neither a definitive account of the progress of the movement for Protestant lay renewal that has come into being, particularly in Europe, since the end of World War II; nor an examination of the theological and sociological foundations which underlie that movement—foundations which are dealt with comprehensively in a number of the books listed in the appendix beginning on page 130. Mine is simply a journalist's report, highlighting features of some of the imaginative ventures through which certain pioneers in Europe and North America are attempting to spark renewal in parish life and to discover new points of contact between the church and the world.

Through the past fifteen years I have been intrigued by occasional word of those ventures as it has showed up from time to time in reports from news correspondents, as well as in more definitive treatments, which arrive at my desk to be processed for appearance in the pages of the *Christian Century.* When I went to Europe in 1958 to cover the annual meetings of the World Council of Churches' Central Committee and related commissions, and to write a series of articles on Protestant church life in that part of the world, I planned that the lay academies in Germany and the Netherlands should come in for a share of attention. Some of my acquaintances discouraged the idea; the academies, they predicted, would doubtless prove to be just another manifestation of an esoteric concern without much potentiality as permanent means of renewal. What I saw proved that prediction wrong. Later, when articles on the German and Dutch academies appeared in the *Century,* readers' response indicated that many North Americans had been likewise intrigued by scattered reports of "something happening" in the lay centers of Europe. So I welcomed the suggestion by the editors of Muhlenberg Press that I expand, to a book, the reports which are necessarily limited in a weekly magazine.

I have not been fortunate enough to have seen in action all the lay centers described in these pages. Information about those which I have not had the opportunity to visit I have gleaned from correspondence and conversation with their leaders, from articles and news reports appearing in the *Century* over the years, and from publications dealing with various aspects of the movement for lay renewal, particularly those issued by the lay centers themselves and by the World Council of Churches' Department on the Laity. To that department I am indebted for permission to reproduce from its booklet *Signs of Renewal,* as revised in 1957, many of the listings in the directory beginning on page 125. I particularly appreciate the forbearance and hospitality of members of the staffs of the lay centers in Germany, the Netherlands, Sweden, and Switzerland who took time out from their busy schedules to show a visitor from the United States their programs in action, and to help her gain an understanding of why those programs exist. And I am grateful to Dr. Walter Leibrecht, of the Evanston Ecumenical Institute, for his helpful suggestions and criticisms during preparation of the manuscript.

M.F.

CONTENTS

INTRODUCTION

Not long ago the Swedish people were surprised to read that a world survey of religions revealed theirs to be the most "Christian" nation on earth. Why? Because ninety-eight per cent of its people are members of the Christian church! The realistic Swedes found in the revelation ground for rueful amusement rather than for pride. True, unless he is one of the nation's small minority of Jews and Roman Catholics, every Swede is considered a member of the state (Lutheran) church at birth, and he remains so until he dies or unless he takes the seldom-resorted-to step of declaring himself "outside the church." But the average Swede—prosperous, healthy, self-reliant—looks on his church membership simply as an identifying designation, like his citizenship, not as a sign that the Christian faith has meaning for him or that its principles govern his actions.

In another "Protestant" country, England, on Sunday mornings the churches stand invitingly open, but the worshipers inside are likely to be few. Throughout the countryside the ancient church buildings are cherished as monuments but, for the most part, the descendants of the people they once served no longer look to the church for her ministries, and in the pattern of their daily lives they are likely to be unaware of any part played by her teachings. "Of course we are Christians," a Briton told a visiting cousin from America recently. "But the church is outmoded and dead."

In Germany, where over ninety-five per cent of the people are nominal church members—either Protestant or Catholic—ecclesiastical authorities concede that, on an average, only about five per cent of the Protestants attend worship services or take any part whatever in church enterprises. In a densely populated industrial town near Frankfort on the Main, an iconoclastic pastor conducting an iconoclastic experiment finds that the men he has met while working on a factory assembly line are enthusiastic about the unconventional Bible study and communion services he has organized at a student-mission center in the neighborhood. But they are unresponsive, often frankly antagonistic, when he suggests that they pursue their newly found interest within their parish churches. "What does the church care about people like us?" they ask. Their prejudice has grown out of their long-held view that the church is strictly a bourgeois preserve.

Said a prominent Italian recently about the situation in his own country: "The church has great political influence, but its ability to motivate the daily actions and decisions of the average Italian is definitely on the decrease." Traveling north from Rome on the Sunday after the death of Pope Pius XII, we stopped at the little town of San Gimignano, famous for its ancient towers, walls, and churches. Inside a large central church a special service was being held for the late pontiff, whose body that October day lay in state in St. Peter's. Perhaps twenty people—older women and a few young girls—knelt in the pews. But outside, in the town square, scores of men stood shoulder to shoulder, earnestly gesticulating, their voices rising and falling in a Niagara of sound. We asked the local guide what they were discussing: the pope's death, perhaps? or politics? She laughed. "Oh no. When Italian men talk together nowadays you can be sure it has nothing to do with religion, probably not with politics. Just now the grape harvest is about ready, and they're discussing where the best deal can be made."

In France, another nominally Roman Catholic country, realistic priests acknowledge that the church has completely lost touch with the working classes. Still, the hierarchy whistles in the dark by citing baptismal statistics, and churchmen bow to a Vatican order putting an end to the imaginative worker-priest movement in which certain perceptive parish pastors donned laborer's garb and went to work in industry for a part of every day in an attempt to reforge ties with working men. Meanwhile, communism continues to have an appeal for many of the workers, and anticlericalism increases in all ranks of society. In eastern Europe, the Christian churches exist only as they are careful not to overstep the restricting bounds set for their activities by the communist regimes; and individual Christians who insist on putting allegiance to their faith before political obligations risk at the very least their means of livelihood, at the most their personal security.

Across the Atlantic, in the United States and Canada, the churches seem at first glance to be flourishing beyond all reasonable expectations, even while the state of public morality declines. On Sunday mornings the pews are filled. But serious questions are being asked about the quality of that large church attendance. It has been suggested that a poll asking for frank answers to questions about why people go to church might bring forth some surprising reasons. There is no doubt that for many the worship services provide inspiration and welcome guidance; but for others, unaware of the implications of the faith they profess, the church and its services are often judged by material standards only. I have heard a businessman explain that he attends a particular church because there he can associate with "some of the biggest men in the city," and "you'll never find riff-raff in *our* pews"; further, "our pastor is not the kind who gets up in the pulpit and tries to tell us how to run our businesses during the week." More typical than is readily acknowledged is this remark by the chairman of a pulpit committee: "We are looking for a safe man; one who won't stir things up too much. People come to church to forget their troubles and find comfort in pleasant sermons, with a little humor on the side if possible." And in the accolade offered by one politician is to be found the core of what many concerned observers identify as the dilemma faced by the American churches: "The one institution we can't do without in this country is the church, because it helps preserve the American way of life, because it is our best defense against communism." If that is all—if that represents the public image of why the church is to be valued—there is ground for the charge that the American churches have become so identified with the mores of the society in which they exist that they hesitate to challenge the things that are wrong with that society. They most assuredly are not being ignored or opposed by the secular world, but they may be victims of an even deadlier treatment: patronization.

Varied echoes, these, of situations which have led to the realization on both sides of the Atlantic that renewal is called for in the life of the churches. Historically, calls for renewal have been sounded when evidence mounted that the essence of the Christian faith was being smothered by the church's over-concern with externals. The responses have come in succeeding waves: the monastic movement in the early Middle Ages which preserved a core of integrity and devotion in the face of dilution and, at the end of the period, rescue of the movement itself from abuses and corruption; the Reformation which reintroduced the essential gospel shorn of the worldly accretions which accompany political power and preferment; the counter-Reformation that sought to correct certain abuses which had played a part in inspiring the Protestant separation; the revival movements in eighteenth century Germany and England and nineteenth century America; the missionary enterprises of the past two centuries; the ecumenical movement of today.

All have been efforts to make the gospel a more vital force in people's lives, to communicate its essentials more effectively.

Today the charge is made that at the present stage of Western history the voice of the Christian church has been, to a considerable extent, either stilled through her own inaction in the face of new demands and new needs, or rendered irrelevant through her desire to conform, to please. At any rate, it is said, she has in many respects ceased to matter where she should matter most: in those areas of life where the laity, the "whole people of God," spend their working hours. In Europe, the need is to forge anew long-broken ties between church and world; in North America, to establish among laymen a realization of what the church is and to make clear what she is not, thus freeing her to sound the prophetic voice that would justify her existence as the channel for the message of redemption.

The forces which have brought about the predicament of the church that seeks to relate herself to the world of today may be identified. In the intellectual world, it is pointed out, the triumphs of science through the past two centuries have led many to conclude that because traditional concepts of the physical nature of the universe have been cast aside, traditional concepts of the spiritual nature of man are also candidates for discard; increasingly, man has been glorified as the master of his fate. Yet along with the recent crescendo of developments which enable man to manipulate the physical world, have come unprecedented fears lest man destroy his own potential for existence. In the face of those fears the church is being challenged to help men find answers to questions posed by new concepts of the world they live in. Pointing out that science, hitherto confident of its competence, now wonders whether it can control the forces it has unleashed, an atomic scientist complains that men of religion, who should be the ones to take over and provide solutions to such questions as why we are here and where we are going, seem as unable as the questioners to provide answers that will stand the tests of pertinence and intelligibility.

"The new world is here," declares a community of Christians seeking to discover ways of relating faith to life in an American university environment. "It is not going to go away. . . . We can, indeed, hide from it and suffer the consequences. But the question of integrity and faith is: How are we to live within it? How can we be human beings through it? How are we to respond to it creatively? How can we be men of faith before it?"[1] In seeking to answer that question, the church is challenged to do more than echo the cry of the questioner or repeat dogmatic responses from the past.

In the social realm, too, forces have operated to estrange the laity from the church as an institution. The humanitarian impulse that, through the nineteenth century, issued in legislation to improve the physical welfare of mankind, doubtless had its inception in the Christian gospel; but in many countries the church, channel for that gospel, let herself be counted out of movements for reform. Indeed, in many instances she gave the impression that her sympathies lay with those who would keep social conditions as they were. When wars came, the church which had preached peace and brotherhood became an ally of the warring forces, and men who had found in her message the source of their determination to oppose violence were repelled by her hypocrisy. Meanwhile, with the onward march of industrialization, men's workaday lives became increasingly governed by the factory whistle, their welfare dependent on distant forces few could comprehend or analyze. Workers on the assembly lines had no illusions about being masters of their fate, yet they hungered for some meaning in the increasingly mechanical, impersonal environment that encompassed them. But the church continued her parochial existence, unaware that around her people's lives were no longer parochial. In Europe particularly, as industrialization advanced, she became ever more bourgeois, concerned to preserve bourgeois values. In time, much

[1] "Breakthrough," *Letter to Laymen* (journal of the Christian Faith-and-Life Community, Austin, Texas), Vol. VI, No. 3 (November, 1959).

of her effort came to be expended on preserving herself as an institution, particularly in those countries where she served as an arm of a state governed by pragmatic, increasingly socialistic regimes. She continued to do commendable works of charity, but more and more—except in isolated ventures undertaken by unconventional (and often unapproved of) individuals—she exhibited scant concern for the ills of the new industrial society which made those charitable works necessary. Near the end of the first half of the twentieth century a French pastor described the church in this way: "She has let herself be imprisoned little by little in her own fortress, forgetting her mission of conquest. Instead of being a community, the church too often has become a pulpit and a congregation. Then the congregation has become sparser, and in many cases there finally remains only the pulpit. . . . The church must go out into the world, live with men, study their problems, and seek with them the solutions which do not result from conformity with the world but from submission to the will of God. . . . The church can have authority only by coming out of her isolation and making the world's distress her own."[2]

In North America the movement toward intense industrialization came more slowly, and the estrangement between church and people resulting from its impact was less severe. Then, as industrialization and urbanization accelerated and social wrongs appeared in their train, a dynamic movement arose in the Protestant churches which considered concern for the righting of those wrongs a primary obligation. Later, when evidence multiplied that the righting of social wrongs alone could not meet man's greatest needs, churchmen's thoughts turned to the center of their faith. They became convinced that, as the channel for the gospel, the church must make greater efforts to minister to the whole man, to man in his workaday life and in his innermost spiritual wonderings.

---

[2] Jean Bosc. Quoted in an interview in "Laymen Are Christians, Too!" an editorial by Harold E. Fey, *Christian Century,* Vol. LXV, No. 33 (August 18, 1948), pp. 823-24.

Today, on both sides of the Atlantic, a new concern for renewal of the life of the churches has arisen. It is not marked, as often in the past, by efforts to form new denominations free of traditional encumbrances; rather, it is accompanied by an impulse toward unity. Its most characteristic manifestation is the revival of a concept of the laity as the primary agency through which the church witnesses in the world.

This concept of the role of the laity has been set forth by a leader of one of several ventures in which churchmen are seeking to recover for the present day the timeless implications of the Christian gospel: "[Christianity] *is a movement of the people . . . living the life of Christ in the world.* . . . Buildings, private worship, ministry, and theology are all essential, but only as aids to men's living of the Christian life. When they become the guardians of religion, something has gone very far wrong. We have forgotten that the church is a lay movement. When things have got too appallingly bad, there has always been a protest. The movement of protest has always been against the 'religionizing' of the faith. They have been efforts to break out into the open air and to get back to some kind of obedience in daily life. These protests have always been essentially lay; however surprising this may appear in the light of what they afterwards became. . . . Today we indeed need a new protest—to assert that what matters is what we do *in the world*. . . . The power of the laity is the power of the Church. The power of the laity is the index of the power of the Church—and their powerlessness the index of the powerlessness of the Church. But when we speak of the power of the Church we must be sure what we mean. There is the power of the Church which the world sees, and which Church folk are so often concerned about. By it they mean the authority of the Church to dominate the lives of men. . . . Sometimes we talk as if it were this power or authority that we wanted to increase. Sometimes, when the Church talks about the greater use of laymen, she seems to mean that she wants to use them out in the world to increase her power in this kind of way. . . . The real power of the Church is something quite different. And if we want to make clear that we are talking of this quite different thing, then perhaps we should talk about *the power of the laity* and not about the power of the Church. For we do not mean the power of an Institution, we mean the power of men and women to affect the life of the world, as Jesus did, by their lives in the world, by love and at the cost of suffering. . . . [A] reason for our fear of action and for our desire to slip back into religious exercises and 'Church work' is that the problems that we see as facing us are new and immense and terrifying. It's much easier to decide to go to Church more regularly or to teach in the Sunday School. Ultimately the power of the laity is a question of our faith. It is a question of our getting back . . . to the basic teaching of the New Testament that God has acted in a man and therefore acts in men—in people like us."[3]

In the years since two world wars shocked the "Christian" West into the realization that within its own borders demonic forces could arise—forces embodying the antithesis of the virtues it professed—a number of pilot ventures arising from this concept of the laity have been initiated. In a variety of ways they seek to discover means of achieving renewal within the churches and of establishing communication between church and secular world. In the pages that follow, an attempt will be made to describe, in informal fashion, some of those ventures. They differ in method, depending on environment, need, and specific purpose. But in all there exists a remarkable similarity in the underlying concern that brought them into being, and in the goals toward which they strive.

---

[3] Ralph Morton, "The Church Is a Lay Movement," *Christian Comment* (Thomas Bray Bookshop, London), No. 14 (November, 1959), pp. 2, 3.

I

SWEDEN: CULTURAL REPENETRATION

Pioneer among the organizations that today are deliberately seeking to foster a more creative encounter between church and culture is the Sigtuna Foundation *(Sigtunastiftelsen)* in Sweden. It had its inception in a movement arising within the state (Lutheran) church of Sweden in the early part of the present century. In those years, when the cultural life of the nation was seething with new ideas, new conceptions of the universe and of man's destiny, the church stood apart from the debate, tied still to the semantics of a bygone era, to the letter rather than the spirit of the Bible, to a dogmatic approach to issues, unaware that the nation's life was sweeping on without her. But voices within the church began to plead for an approach that would take into account that God's Word is not contained in stone tablets but is written also in history, and that his love pervades all of life.

Those voices found an echo among university students allied

with the Student Christian Movement.[1] The students coined a watchword, "The Swedish People—God's People," and went out two by two into the streets and byways, challenging intellectual doubters with their concept of a gospel that has the power to permeate and recreate all phases of life. At first the "Young Church Movement," as it came to be called, met stubborn opposition from reactionary forces at the head of the state church. But it persisted, not so much an entity as an emphasis—a freshened outlook and aim. In succeeding decades it was echoed particularly in the vision and endeavors of certain of the church's leaders who had participated in the movement during their student days.

One of those leaders was Manfred Björkquist, who had gone to the University of Uppsala with no intention of entering the ministry of the church. In fact, his pastor father—mourning the impotence of the church in the face of a changing culture—had advised, "I doubt that there will even be a church for you to serve within twenty years." But the son's experience in the Student Christian Movement was decisive, and he threw himself wholeheartedly into the struggle being waged by the Young Church Movement. Later he took a theological degree; in time, became bishop of Stockholm.

In 1915, Björkquist appealed to his coworkers: "Ours has been a good movement. But we must implement it into something permanent. We need a center, a place where people of all kinds can come to study and confer, where our own ideas can become crystallized."

Sigtuna was the result. The name comes from the village which lies along a curve of the northern shoreline of Lake Mäler, whose southern reaches border the city of Stockholm. It is an ancient townsite, created as the nation's capital early in the eleventh century by Olaf Sköttkonung, the first Christian king of Sweden, and it was destined to play a leading role in the struggle between the

[1] This movement, with roots in mid-nineteenth century England, gained admission into Uppsala in 1901, and Lund in 1902.

new faith and paganism in that northern land. Two hundred years later it became the site of the first Dominican monastery in Sweden. Decay had set in with the transfer of the capital to Stockholm about the middle of the twelfth century, and with repeated pillage by Estonian pirates. The death blow was struck to the town as a center of early Christian activity by the closing of all monasteries in Sweden in 1527. Within the limits of Sigtuna today stand intriguing relics of days long past: ruined church towers and courtyards, runic stones, cairns marking the final resting places of priests and vikings.

THE SIGTUNA FOUNDATION

Today the village is again the center of a Christian enterprise known far beyond the nation's borders. Just outside its limits, up a pine-clad hillside spotted by occasional moss-laced outcroppings of the underlying granite, climb the Sigtuna Foundation's buildings, the paved courtyards, slit-windowed towers, and arched passageways giving on to formal rose plantings—all strangely reminiscent of Mediterranean lands.

From the beginning, the foundation's purpose has been not to convert men and women to particular viewpoints, but to "serve with the whole purpose of serving." Immediately after the first building was dedicated, in 1917, invitations went out to clergymen and laymen to come to confer on the problem posed by the estrangement from the church of so many of the Swedish people. Next an opportunity was offered university students to come together at Sigtuna with delegations of laborers so that each group could interpret its particular "world" to the other. In the early 1920's the world of labor was unknown to the universities and their students, and the effects of that and similar conferences which succeeded it were far-reaching. Today such meetings are no longer unusual, nor are they so urgent; the working man is no stranger to members of Sweden's academic circles, and students confront his problems not only in daily life but in the university curricula. Nevertheless, biannual conferences at Sigtuna still offer each student generation an opportunity to meet with representatives of labor and explore the relation of the Christian gospel to industrial and social problems, or some other aspect of the cultural scene with which both groups are concerned.

Shortly after Sigtuna was established, a crisis arose in labor-management relations which threatened to create a permanent schism in Sweden's national life. Management had not yet acknowledged that labor had a right to any voice in economic affairs; nor was that right conceded by the government or by the church. For some time the Sigtuna staff had been devoting study to the increasing fragmentation of Swedish life into groups delineated by vocation, social class, and ideology; and a number of conferences at the center had discussed the threat to national welfare posed by such estrangement. Now the foundation's leaders proposed that representatives of labor and management be invited to come to the center and "talk out" their differences in a neutral atmosphere, where the religious framework would be unobtrusive and non-compulsory but nevertheless present in general feeling and opportunities to take part in worship. As a result of two conferences held at Sigtuna, labor-management tensions were eased and the crisis resolved. The public began to recognize that out of the "spirit of Sigtuna" (the phrase became a slogan) concrete results benefiting all segments of the population might ensue. Sigtuna lays no claim to having introduced the leaven that has led through the years to increasingly good relations between labor and management in Sweden, but many impartial observers insist that such is the case. Those early industrial relations conferences were the first of many of like nature that met later at the center. And they are still a feature of the program, bringing together two or three times a year, from many fields of endeavor, leaders concerned about the personal implications of advancing industrialization.

The labor-management discussions are only one phase of a many-sided program in the quiet, spacious buildings on the hillside above Lake Mälar. Opportunity is provided for encounter beteen clergymen and physicians, clergymen and teachers, clergymen and artists, and so on through the spectrum of modern vocation. And there are meetings between clergymen and clergymen, physicians and physicians, artists and artists.

Olov Hartman, present director of the center, explains that the essential need of the church today is for clergymen and laymen to meet on neutral ground to learn from each other's sphere of experience. When the gates are opened so opinions, experiences, philosophies, and traditions can meet freely, the result is not a conquering of each other's views or even a compromise, but an understanding and an ability to see one's own position with new clarity and a critical eye. An example of such encounter was the meeting arranged at Sigtuna between pastors and physicians shortly after the first Kinsey report on sex attitudes and practices was published. The Swedish public was predicting that the pastors would come out in angry denunciation of the report and denial that the conditions it reported existed. At the conference the physicians were agreeably surprised to discover that the pastors were ready to face up to the implications of the report, were concerned to discover the root of the problem of excessive sexual indulgence (admittedly a serious one in Sweden), and were eager to obtain from the medical profession insights which might help them develop a creative approach to the question. Since then the physicians have called for more opportunities to confer with the pastors on mutual concerns.

Particularly productive have been the encounters at Sigtuna between clergymen, authors, and journalists gathered from all over Scandinavia. And the welcome sign is out for writers and scholars who are interested in living at the guest house for a time in order to make use of the foundation's extensive library. There the 62,000-odd volumes, the 225 current magazines both Swedish and foreign, the magazine files dating back to 1915, and the almost one million newspaper clippings constitute what the Sigtuna staff describes as a "conference in miniature." In the library tower, off the winding staircase, are quiet cubicles equipped with shelves, desks, and chairs for the exclusive use of the researchers. Each year the Swedish Author's Society makes awards to two authors, providing them the chance to spend time working among the library's riches. The center does not require that the visitors be engaged in religious writing; winners of the awards one year recently happened to be a Roman Catholic and an agnostic. At Sigtuna Erik Linder wrote part of his monumental history of twentieth-century Swedish literature; by doing so, he estimated, he was able to complete the work a year earlier than would otherwise have been possible.

Nor are researchers the only nonconference people who are welcome to enjoy the hospitality of the guest house and library. When the facilities are not otherwise in use, men and women from all over Sweden often choose to spend their holidays in relaxation and renewal at Sigtuna, sharing the community's program of daily worship, walking in the pine woods, reading or conversing in the comfortable common-rooms. Some come from abroad; at Sigtuna, one July, I met a London businessman and his wife—once refugees from Hitler's Vienna—who return year after year for a week's "renewal" on the hillside above Lake Mälar.

Not all the conferences at Sigtuna involve clerical-lay encounter. Some, young Pär Olofsson of the staff told me, are given over simply to discussions by laymen who wish to explore the "reasons why" behind some situation or problem with which they are mutually concerned. "But they all carry out one of the purposes of the foundation," he told me. "That is, to foster a 'cultural diaconate' within the church. If people are facing difficult problems, the church ought to find out about those problems—not to give dogmatic answers, but to listen, first, and then try to help; but humbly, not arrogantly, all the time realizing that just possibly she herself may be wrong in this particular case. In all such conferences, the Christian view is set forth as clearly as possible, usually by a convinced layman who can put that view into terms people can understand. In that way we don't have people shying away from discussion and feeling, 'Now here come the pastors to tell us what we should think.' In a way, you can say that each problem dealt with here comes around without conscious design to have theological implications. And we trust that, because this is so, God is pointing the way to reconciliation. The essential point is that things are not 'managed' with that end in view but, nevertheless, it happens."

At times Sigtuna is host to meetings involving only ecclesiastical personnel. One of its buildings, down in the village, houses the Scandinavian Ecumenical Institute, founded in 1940 as a clearing house for the interrelated interests of the northern churches, state and free, and as an agency through which they can communicate with churches in other parts of the world. The foundation's hillside facilities are available to participants in the meetings and conferences sponsored by the institute.

Still other "church" enterprises have their focus at Sigtuna. In one of the most recent ventures, opportunity has been provided for conversation between young men studying in the theological faculties of Uppsala, Lund, and Turku (the Swedish-speaking seminary in Finland). Between those faculties has existed a state amounting almost to ideological warfare, and there is not much anticipation that the somewhat obscure arguments will be resolved to the satisfaction of older theologians. But in their meetings at Sigtuna the younger men have discovered that what separates them is not so much basic principles as semantics, and there are hopes that the differences may some day be reconciled. Thus, at Sigtuna, encounter may lead to the bridging not only of rifts between church and culture but of gulfs within the church as well.

Overall, the emphasis at the center in recent years tends to be slanted more toward encounters with leaders in Sweden's general cultural life than, as in earlier days, with people from the industrial and social milieu. In part, this development stems from the fact that material well-being has been so markedly improved with the smooth functioning of the welfare state; in part, one surmises, from

Director Hartman's own deep interest in matters pertaining to the arts, particularly in exploring the function of the arts as liturgical aids to worship. The center has close ties with the new experimental use of the drama in Sweden. Each summer Sigtuna is host to young people from the national network of drama circles that constitute the Foundation for Liturgy and Drama. Rigorous sessions provide training in methods and technique for representatives of the more than eighty drama circles working in Student Christian Movement groups on the university campuses and in scores of local churches for revival of the medieval practice of presenting eternal religious truths through the media of voice, gesture, and dance. Annually, in August, a two-week cycle of liturgical dramas, many of them written by Hartman himself, is presented in the tree-mottled moonlight flooding the courtyard "church" whose altar is carved into the outer wall of the tower that rises above the Sigtuna chapel. Throughout the year the circles' activities are correlated in a headquarters office with a full-time director, located—naturally enough—at Sigtuna. One hears that from the seed planted by these circles has sprung the secular Swedish theater's new-found interest in presenting plays with religious overtones—concrete evidence of what sometimes can ensue from creative church-world encounter.

SIGTUNA'S SCHOOLS

One of Sigtuna's hillside buildings is occupied by a "people's college," as the Swedish institutions patterned after the Danish folk schools introduced by N.F.S. Grundtvig in the nineteenth century are known. The difference between the usual Swedish people's college and the Sigtuna school is that, in the latter, a religious orientation is present; religion is taught in addition to the usual courses in literature, history, science, arts, crafts, and music. The school offers a pedagogically liberal two- or three-year course designed to open the gates of general knowledge to young people who, for one reason or another, have had to leave school at the elementary level. The coexistence on a single hillside of both the college and the institute is due to the fortunate circumstance that the Church of Sweden was ready to build a people's college just when Manfred Björkquist sounded his appeal for a church-world center. Björkquist was the college's first headmaster. Now retired from his post as bishop of Stockholm, he returns to Sigtuna for the summer holiday period; there he delights in playing the organ for the daily vesper services.

Some ten years after the people's college and lay center were established, a "humanistic school" was set up under auspices of the Sigtuna Foundation, but entirely separate from the other projects. A private boarding school, whose curriculum provides a classical education, it is housed in impressive Grecian-style buildings on top of a hill which rises steeply from the lake shore a mile or so beyond the lay center. Many of its 450 students are children of Swedish diplomats or businessmen who live abroad. Each year thirty or so students, however, attend on scholarships assigned by the church.

Though management of the Sigtuna Foundation is in the hands of an independent seven-member committee, the primate of the Church of Sweden is the official "visitor" and may take part in all committee deliberations if he wishes to do so. The charter specified that certain church organizations and the Student Christian Movement should be represented on the committee, as well as the dean and chapters of, alternately, the dioceses of Lund and Uppsala.

CHURCH-SPONSORED INSTITUTIONS

The Church of Sweden sponsors other people's colleges, mostly on a diocesan basis. No other, however, is associated with a guest house or a conference center. The conference-center phase of Sigtuna's program is echoed to a certain degree in a number of diocesan study centers, usually located in a "natural beauty spot." Many of them have stemmed from diocesan youth programs, for which a central conference site is recognized to be a must. Occasionally one or the other is host to conferences between churchmen and representatives of occupational groups which have made contact with each other at Sigtuna and wish to continue the encounter on a regional basis, drawing a wider circle of participants into the discussion. But as might be expected from their official relation to the dioceses, the regional centers are mainly at the service of official church organizations interested in training laymen to do specific tasks for the church. Though opportunity for church-world encounter is thus limited, many Swedish churchmen feel that even this limited opportunity has within it the seeds for future growth.

In two institutions related to the Church of Sweden administratively as is the Sigtuna Foundation, worship plays a prominent part. They are the St. Katharine's and the Hjälmseryd foundations. St. Katherine's, at Sparreholm, not far from Stockholm, was founded by the Women's Church Council and the Church Board for Voluntary Service as a retreat house and meeting and communications center for church and secular women's organizations. Its director, Dr. Margit Sahlin, was one of the woman theologians eligible for ordination under the dispensation whereby the Swedish parliament (therefore the will of the people) obliged the state church to sanction the service of women as clergy. The primate of the Church of Sweden himself performed the ceremony of ordination for Dr. Sahlin, one of the first three women to be ordained in the church. That action, taken in the spring of 1960, brought loud protest from a group of church officials and pastors unalterably opposed to the ordination of women but apparently not bent on producing a split in the church over the matter, as at first was threatened. Among the opponents are a number of men who in their youth were active in the Young Church Movement and who, in recent years, have become increasingly "high church," with a deep interest in liturgical revival. The Hjälmseryd Foundation developed out of the Swedish liturgical revival; it oversees a community dedicated to furthering liturgical research and practice, and its program centers in a restored medieval church in the province of Småland.

Related to the state church in somewhat the same manner as the above foundations is the Geijer School, a new institution in the province of Värmland, at which musical activities are stressed and where the program, still in the process of formation, will provide services similar to those at the Sigtuna guest house and people's college, but on a smaller scale. The school is named for Erik Geijer who, in early nineteenth century Sweden, advocated reforms in church and culture somewhat on the order of those called for in Denmark by N.F.S. Grundtvig.

All these ventures are visible signs of the concern and determination of a nucleus of her members that the Church of Sweden should witness more clearly to the gospel, become a more vital force in the wide unredeemed areas of the nation's life. As perhaps the most completely "established" church of Protestantism, she has traditionally been satisfied to be "the state performing its religious function," the visible sign of God's relation to a political entity. But except in the more remote rural areas she has ceased to be much more than a symbol. Meanwhile, many of the welfare services for which people once looked to the church have been assumed by the state. At the same time, underneath the all-pervading well-being and complacency that a workable socialist political system and the absence of devastating warfare have brought to modern Sweden, distressing undercurrents of uneasiness have risen to challenge the church to move out of her self-prescribed niche.

Sweden's many able ecclesiastical leaders are aware that many people are floundering spiritually in the midst of prosperity, in need of the church's ministry. Juvenile delinquency is widespread, the nation's suicide and divorce rates are among the world's highest, the percentage of illegitimate births is climbing, cynicism and a "what of it?" attitude are common, self-interest determines the goals pursued by men and women on many levels of society.

When, in 1951, the Swedish bishops issued a pastoral letter on family life and the associated problems of divorce, adultery, and other social ills, they created a public sensation. Secular protest was vehement; not because of what the bishops said so much as because of their daring to speak out at all on a public issue—something that hadn't happened in recent times. In the situation of estrangement symbolized by that protest, concerned Swedish churchmen recognize a continuing need for new bridges to be flung across the gap between church and people, between religion and culture. Sigtuna, they recognize, is a blueprint pointing the way toward effective construction of such bridges.

II

GREAT BRITAIN: CONCERN FOR "TOTAL" MAN

The young British playwright, in New York for the premiere of his latest play, was explaining why the theme of that play reflects nostalgia for an idealized past, rather than the kind of protest sounded by many of his "angry young man" colleagues. "Young people feel that something has gone wrong," he said. "But they don't know who or what can put it right again. The left wing that attracted them in the thirties doesn't attract them today. But neither does the right. The split atom is not the cause of the unease; it only accelerates it. We suffer from a deeper mental and emotional shake-up that followed the collapse of religious faith. For don't doubt that it has collapsed in England. Man's tragedy in England and much of Europe is that he has lost his faith in God and has found nothing to replace it. I would give anything to believe in God. I go on teaching my three children the old-fashioned virtues—to be decent, honest, truthful, just, kind and generous.

But the day when my oldest child asks me why, I'm sunk. My father had a ready answer: 'Because it's God's plan.' I shall have to tell her that she must seek truth and justice because it will be hell on earth for her if she doesn't. But that is a practical reason, not a moral one."[1]

That the young playwright's cry is neither a thinly disguised boast nor an appeal for sympathy—but an honest plea for answer in terms that make sense today—is just one of many challenges faced by the churches of Great Britain. In England only ten per cent, in Scotland perhaps twenty-five per cent of the people are actively associated with religious institutions. Statistics compiled recently by the established Church of England (Anglican) reveal that of the twenty-six million people who have been baptized under her auspices, only nine million have been confirmed and only 2,348,000 are active in her ongoing life. The free church record is not much different.

Facts such as these have led a minority within the British churches to search for new and potent ways to translate the faith they profess into relevant terms, to demonstrate in concrete actions that the church is anxious to become an effective means of bringing all men into touch with the love of God.

One of the most dynamic of Britain's churchmen, George MacLeod, a pastor of the Church of Scotland, contends that the West has come to the end of an era; that we are confronted by the changed nature of modern man. The concept of the primacy of individual salvation was perhaps plausible, he points out, in an age of individualism. But modern man is becoming "total," and the emotional side of his being, to which that concept appealed, is only one facet of his totality. The thought form in which the gospel is ordinarily preached—quite sincerely and loyally—Dr. MacLeod sees as not really the thought form of modern man. He contends

---

[1] Robert Bolt. In an interview reported by Inez Robb in her column in the Chicago *Daily News,* October 1959 (Copyright, 1959, United Features syn dicate, New York).

that if the appeal of the church is to be productively directed to all aspects of the life of modern man, the church itself must be "turned 'round."

Then, with a rare gift for turning symbol and parable to prophetic use, the Scottish clergyman explains what he means by the "church turned 'round." St. Nicholas Parish Church in Liverpool, he tells us, once stood high above the Mersey, a river busy with commerce; it towered far above the dockyards and busy market place. To enter it, one had to turn his back on river and market place and climb a hill; once inside, he peered at the distant communion table, gloomy in the sparse light seeping through dusty, ancient stained glass. But wartime bombing changed all that. Only the porch and tower remained intact, the ruined walls let in the winds of heaven. Within the ruin an imaginative rector caused a miniature temporary church to be built. But it was "turned 'round," so that large, clear-glass windows looked out on the river and market place. And the communion table stood in the midst of the congregation.[2]

THE IONA COMMUNITY

Moved by his sense of the symbolic, made aware of man's need through years of ministry in a fashionable Edinburgh church, and later in one of the most depressing slums of industrial Glasgow, George MacLeod in 1938 joined with a group of like-minded Scots to found the Iona Community, which seeks to discover, and in its own small way to demonstrate, how the church might actually be "turned 'round" to serve man where he works and lives, how the gospel of the Incarnation might become a living force in every aspect of Scottish life. If the idea the community embodies has not yet permeated throughout the Church of Scotland (Presbyterian), under whose auspices it now operates, the experiment has at least planted seeds of awareness in that Reformed communion, while

[2] George F. MacLeod, *We Shall Rebuild* (Glasgow: Iona Community, publisher), pp. 12-13.

throughout Protestantism reflections of its significance have been caught and pondered.

The community centers on the tiny, craggy island of Iona off Scotland's rugged western coast. It was to Iona, in the sixth century, that St. Columba and a little band of companions came from Ireland to erect a church, and from there that they set out in bands of twelve to convert pagan Scotland to Christianity. As the years passed, the Celtic church, in fellowship with Rome but not subservient to her, declined. In the eleventh century Iona again flourished as a center of Christian enterprise with the erection of a Benedictine monastery on the island. Then monasteries were outlawed in the land, and for years the old walls gradually crumbled away, leaving their stone foundations, however, sturdy and foursquare. Late in the nineteenth century the Duke of Argyle, whose property the island had become, entrusted it to the Church of Scotland, expressing the hope that the rocky bit of land again might become a place of service for all of Christendom. In the first decade of the twentieth century the old abbey church was restored.

By 1938, George MacLeod, ministering to the sorely beset people in his industrial parish in Glasgow, had become convinced that a serious deficiency hobbled the church's approach to modern man. As he put it recently, "The tragedy of our day is the divorce between the sacred and the secular, and an imagined dichotomy between religion and science. Our technical achievements have been allowed to outrun our spiritual resources. Men have failed to realize the relevance of the faith to their responsibilities and decisions in their work and public life. The faith has become an individual affair for men to take or leave. The corrosive power of communism flourishes because it is a total philosophy, but it is based on the lie that the ultimate reality is material. Scientists now declare that the material and the spiritual are indivisible. We must recover a total philosophy that declares this truth to burn at the very core of every activity and discovery of modern man. Only then can the church meet this challenge."

Observing the estrangement from the church apparent in members of his Glasgow parish, Dr. MacLeod recalled that the pioneers of the Celtic church, combining work, worship, and preaching on the island of Iona, had proceeded intuitively on the assumption that the spiritual and the material, this life and the next, eternity and now, were intertwined like the dual strands of the endless rope found so often in Celtic design. He saw a chance to translate symbol into reality by proceeding consciously on the same assumption. From the Church of Scotland he obtained permission to continue the work of restoration on Iona: rebuilding the structures on the three sides of the abbey cloister attached to the church, as well as the smaller outlying houses. Then he resigned his pulpit and gathered together a little group of people resolved to undergo a disciplined life of work and worship and, thus prepared, to engage in a crusade to make the Christian faith operative in the whole structure of Scottish life.

Through the years since then a dedicated community has spent the summer months on windswept Iona: graduate theological students who "contract into membership" for two years' training in addition to their standard course; artisans who contribute their skills to direct the restoration of buildings; ministers and laymen from all over Scotland who, during the rest of the year, carry on their regular vocations.

Demonstrating that insight comes not so much from theory as from experience, the daily round of activity on the island follows a pattern designed to symbolize the importance of the Christian faith in the whole of man's life. Members of the summer community, and those who come for only short periods of time, share a communal life. They work at building tasks and housekeeping chores; their labor has meant that two-thirds of the cloister buildings have been restored, providing living quarters to replace the wooden huts that sheltered the original eight members of the community—four pastors and four laymen. They take part in a disciplined regimen of prayer and worship. The communal worship service is simple but meaningful; intercession is personal, specific; an effort is made to discover from earlier practice and put to modern use such liturgical elements as will make the significance of the sacraments more clear and immediate. Dr. MacLeod points out that in the early days of Christian worship on Iona the communion table was central; but, with the ascendance of the priestly, a screen was erected to separate the table from the lay worshipers. In the restoration at Iona the table has again become central. During the communion service the minister stands behind the table in the midst of the congregation. The loaves of bread, baked by the people themselves, are borne in by members of the community in procession, broken and consecrated in the sight of all. Thus, symbolically, the essence of the Iona idea: Incarnation in the *whole* of the people's lives.

Much time is devoted to studying the modern social and religious scene and developing new concepts of service. Members of the community seek together to discover what means can best be employed to establish communication with the people in Scotland's industrial areas, in the vast new housing developments, in the busy streets and remote byways. For when the summer is over the artisans go back to their jobs on the mainland, there to practice daily the "rule" of Iona they have resolved to make their own. The clerical members of the community spread out two by two in a "team ministry" that takes them, under assignment by the Church of Scotland, to all corners of the country—sometimes abroad. A few of the recent theological seminary graduates find their place of service in the Iona Youth Trust, endowed by a friend of the community to operate a play-pray-study center for young people in industrial Glasgow, to support student chaplaincies, to bring boys and girls to Iona for conferences and camps, and to conduct various other enterprises of benefit to the country's youth.

In their industrial program on the mainland, the Iona Community members seek to establish groups of workers and managers who try to work out techniques whereby, on the basis of Christian convictions, they can help solve problems of industry and politics. In Glasgow, the Iona Foundation operates Community House, where opportunity is offered people caught up in the pressures of urban living and occupations to find an outlet for their energies and their concerns. A wide range of study courses is offered—on everything from the meaning of the faith to the impact on people's lives of drama and film. In addition, training is provided in youth leadership, the duties of congregational elders, and service through parish missions. People who come to Community House are continually encouraged to take active part in political life and civic enterprises, and preparation for such participation is available at the center. Traditionally, such encouragement has had no place in the life of the average Scottish congregation.

Each summer, in a project centering in Community House, theological students take jobs in shipbuilding yards and steel plants; meanwhile living together, sharing experiences and insights. But with all the activities that crowd the center in Glasgow, the staff realizes that mere instruction and service are not enough. Therefore, it is always trying to discover ways of relating newly interested lay people to the corporate worship of the congregations in their home parishes; there, it maintains, is the gap it hopes some day to bridge completely.

In 1960, twenty-two years after it was launched, the Iona Community counted, in its central operating core, 140 full members, plus 575 "associates," men and women who keep the community "rule" of spiritual discipline and attend the winter regional meetings, but are not engaged full time in what amounts to a ministry of evangelism. In addition, a worldwide circle of some five thousand "friends of Iona" engage in some form of personal spiritual discipline and support the venture with regular gifts. These gifts have made possible most of the rebuilding on the island as well as some of the service projects on the mainland. For, though the community is now attached to the Church of Scotland, the relationship is, as Dr. MacLeod puts it, "for discipline, not for rations." And the relationship does not mean that non-Presbyterians are excluded from participation in the community. Indeed, representatives of all ecclesiastical traditions are welcome to take part in the conferences and other activities at Iona, and many are represented among the "friends." Not long ago, a Greek Orthodox celebration of the Mysteries took place in the abbey church, with Anglicans and Presbyterians present.

The community's concern is not limited to Scotland alone. A recent proclamation by the "Men of Iona," issued in connection with an appeal on behalf of the foundation, declares the intention to "recover the social significance of the sacraments." And it adds: "The 'war on want' will never be won save by Christian principle. The Sacrament teaches us how to share Bread . . . get into politics—all parties—to deal with the whole man and not just the soul; to feed the hungry and to clothe the naked that the 'least of the nations' may be fed, lest the West should come into Judgment now in this present time."

Not all members of the Church of Scotland (of which Dr. MacLeod spent one term as moderator) are enthusiastic about the Iona experiment. That Dr. MacLeod is a pacifist has nothing to do with any lack of enthusiasm, for within the community is to be found every shade of attitude on the question of the church and war. It is rather that the venture is unconventional in a land where most procedures are conventional, where the "kirk" way of functioning and the "kirk" attitude to public life have long been set in an unchanging pattern. But as evidences mount that neither routine forms of congregational practice nor emotional appeals are going to cause the Scots to turn for motivation to their traditional faith, the idea Iona embodies remains to prick the conscience. Something more is needed, and to an increasing number of Scottish churchmen it is coming to seem that Iona may be pointing the way.

OTHER BRITISH MOVEMENTS

The Iona Community is but the most visible sign, impressive in its symbolism and insights, of a stirring of recognition within Great Britain's churches that radical methods are worth trying if the Christian faith is to penetrate a culture in which some lives indicate desperation and protest, others uncaring boredom and indifference.

For several years an organization called the Christian Frontier Council has brought together a small but influential body of British lay men and women engaged in public affairs, business, and the professions. Their purpose is to study together how the Christian faith affects questions they must deal with in their daily occupations, and to view national issues in the light of that faith. Out of the council's experiences and research has come a notable series of widely circulated reports that have exerted a creative influence on British life.

Two of the active participants in the Christian Frontier Council, J. H. Oldham and Kathleen Bliss, are now associated with a unique new venture sponsored by the British Y.M.C.A. Dunford College, as it is called, is housed in a spacious residence on a two-hundred acre estate in Sussex which once was the home of Richard Cobden, noted nineteenth century social reformer. Designed to serve the Christian witness at the policy-making level, the "college" offers opportunity for communication among men in positions of responsibility, men who make vital decisions in Britain's social, economic, or political life. At Dunford, three interrelated endeavors are carried on: discussion of mutual concerns by men engaged in important public and private enterprises; research projects delving into philosophical and religious questions, along with conferences for people interested in and competent to speak on those questions; study of social, political, and industrial developments in Africa, for whose future welfare the government and the churches are deeply and uneasily concerned, even though British colonies there are rapidly becoming independent. Through these varied programs, able and responsible laymen are finding it possible to make a definite impact on national policy; and they themselves are becoming more aware of the insights their faith can offer for developments on the frontiers of social and political life.

In addition to Dunford, the British Y.M.C.A. has, since the end of World War II, established four other colleges whose aim is to help skilled industrial workers discover and understand the relation of their faith to their daily work. To Coleg y Fro (College in the Vale), in southern Wales, industrial firms send outstanding workers between the ages of sixteen and twenty for annual one-week courses over a three-year period. One or another group of workers is in residence at the college every week in the year. There they are helped to put their personal concerns into words and, through discussion, reading, and consultation, to see those concerns in the light of wider relationships. The staff maintains contact with the boys during the time between their annual visits to the college, and they are encouraged to call on its members for aid or counsel, should the need arise. At Kingsgate College, in Kent, two-week courses plus "refresher" sessions, advanced studies, and reunions are conducted for boys who have completed apprentice training in industry. The aim is to enable them, in part through literary and historical studies, to see higher goals in their jobs than material remuneration, to understand their relationship to society, and to consider the importance of Christian principles in their daily work. A similar aim, utilizing more academic means, is pursued in Y.M.C.A. projects at Cambridge and Durham Universities, where up to ten men at a time from the "junior executive" level in industry are invited to study for a quarter-term under the tutelage of a "Y" staff member, with the privilege of using the universities' resources.

To attend these Y.M.C.A. colleges, workers are granted leave from their jobs by their employers, who also bear the cost of their living expenses. Typically, of the boys who enroll only about one-fourth have been connected with any church. But a survey has revealed that within two years after completing their courses a substantial number of the uncommitted have formed a church relationship.

MOVEMENTS WITHIN THE CHURCHES

Two church-world colleges—William Temple, at Rugby, and Moor Park, at Farnham in Surrey—were established by groups within the Church of England but have, on their boards and in their student bodies, free churchmen as well as Anglicans. William Temple College, named for the late Archbishop of Canterbury who was a pioneer leader in the ecumenical movement, was founded by churchmen who shared the archbishop's concern that the Christian faith be operative in the field of industry. It offers courses and conferences of varying lengths for people interested in looking at life and work in the light of Christianity. Among the students, only part of whom are church members, are industrial managers, schoolteachers, professional men and women, civic employees, and social welfare workers. Special conferences on "Christian Responsibility in Industry" are held from time to time. One-year divinity courses are available to people in the field of education who wish to explore the religious scene more thoroughly. Theological graduates study at the school in preparation for service in industrial parishes. On the other hand, Moor Park College offers a variety of general adult education courses—in social problems, science, the arts, agriculture, race relations, health—all set against a background of Christian thought, practice, and worship. For committed Christians there are special studies in the bearing of their faith on daily life. In cooperation with Oversea Service, an agency of the British Council of Churches and the Conference of British Missionary Societies, Moor Park conducts special courses of study designed to give men en route to diplomatic or business posts abroad knowledge of the culture and interests of the people among whom they will be living, as well as an appreciation of the Christian tradition they will be assumed to represent.

In certain Anglican parishes clergymen, most of them young, are experimenting with methods of parish renewal in an effort to carry the church into the lives of people who, while nominally members of the Church of England, have long since lost the habit of taking part in her services or depending on her ministries. Sometimes devotions are conducted for a single family at home, sometimes several families are gathered together in a central home for worship. Often communion becomes a part of the worship, with the kitchen table as the center. One of the most widely known of these British "house church" experiments is described by Canon Ernest Southcott, of the parish of Halton in the industrial city of Leeds. In his book, *The Parish Comes Alive,* Canon Southcott tells how during the week his parishioners, clad in their working clothes, meet in a central house in their own neighborhoods for communion services conducted by the local pastor, or for Bible study or discussion of community problems led by one of their own number. The result, in many cases, is that the church's worship and ministries become a part of the people's very lives. Only on Sunday are culminating services held in the parish church.[3]

Somewhat the same idea has been introduced by members of the Iona Community in parishes of the Church of Scotland, with elders leading monthly "house meetings" at which parishioners and their friends discuss local issues, take part in Bible study, and join in informal worship.

Other Anglican clergymen have taken a more radical step; they have gone into industry as regular employees, sharing their fellow workers' experiences and problems, counseling as the need arises, carrying on their own parish duties (usually as vicars) after working hours and on Sundays. They disclaim any intention to form a "movement," sensing that dangers can arise when a rigid pattern is set; their aim is rather to find every possible opportunity to help make the church mean more to workingmen than it now

[3] Ernest W. Southcott, *The Parish Comes Alive* (New York: Morehouse-Gorham, 1956), pp. 44-68.

does. So far their number is few, and their efforts have not always met with official sanction.

It was not always so in Britain, this separation between laboring men and the churches. In the early years of the nation's trade-union movement an amazing number of the leaders were lay preachers, some even ordained ministers, from the free churches. It has been said that the early trade-union leaders gained in Methodist "meetings" the skill in oratory which made their appeals to the rank and file of labor effective. But once the movement was crystallized, such men were seldom found in positions of leadership. And there are few links left on any level.

Today certain free church ministers are attempting to reforge the broken links. One such is William Gowland who, in 1954, left a prominent Methodist pulpit to become pastor of a broken-down congregation in a densely industrial district of London, and to serve as chaplain in ten factories nearby. He discovered at once that his greatest lack was real understanding of the conditions under which his parishioners and their neighbors worked, and of the problems that beset them. His probings led him to the discovery that, as he puts it, laboring men have not deserted Christianity; they have simply lost patience with the other-worldly expression of Christianity encountered in most of the churches. Gowland believes that the church has not only failed to understand the problems of men and women who are bound to the treadmill of modern industry, but has not yet discovered how to put her message in terms simple and concrete enough to be applied to situations people meet in factory, mine, and office.

William Gowland acted on his discovery. He set up in his parish an "industrial college" where chaplains, apprentices, experienced workers, and managers study the workings of industry and the problems it poses for human beings. In addition, they are given down-to-earth courses in theology; Gowland is convinced that the issues raised have theological import. In the five years the "college" has been in operation, over three hundred ministers and laymen have completed the course of study; and in 1958 many applicants had to be turned down because of the lack of sufficient facilities. Now the British Methodist Church's Board of Missions is supporting the project, the first of its kind in the denomination, and a committee on industrial evangelism has been set up in each of its districts.

That word "evangelism" bothers Gowland; he would like to see it regain its original noble significance. He says the word has for too long been associated with preaching missions that leave little residue of increased Christian commitment or sound theological understanding. He would have any man who knows why he is a Christian, and who makes a Christian impact on the principles and practices of his vocational group, be considered as engaging in evangelism. And he would have the same concept applied to people whose job or profession involves them in international relationships.

Isolated instances, these, of sincere attempts to bridge the gap of indifference that is acknowledged to stand between Great Britain's churches and large sections of the British public. Unconventional enterprises, for the most part. Against the temptation to write them off as futile, George MacLeod sounded a warning and encouragement when he declared, in the early days of his Iona experiment, "To say that the church, in a day of transition, must be prepared to change some of her methods is not to be impatient but to express confidence in the continued activity of God's Spirit, Who has never failed to speak to His church, and never confines His promptings to the great and wise: but shares out a sufficiency to any little company prepared to move forward in His name, with however many stumbles."[4]

---

[4] MacLeod, *We Shall Rebuild,* p. 1.

III

GERMANY: BUILDING NEW BRIDGES

In no country has the laymen's-center method of search for church renewal had so profuse a flowering in the years since World War II as in Germany, and in no country was renewal so needed.

True, as in Sweden, all but a tiny minority of Germans are nominally church members, Protestant or Roman Catholic; not many have taken the socially disapproved step of declaring themselves "outside" and so not obligated to pay the church tax which the state collects annually along with other income assessments. But Protestants have come to look on their membership in the regional state churches (Lutheran, Union, or Reformed) as they do their citizenship or family lineage. Most of them have their children baptized, some see that they are confirmed; and they look to the church for her ministries at the time of marriage and death. "Four-wheeled Christians," many are called, for they arrive at the church door only by perambulator, marriage coach, or hearse. On a national average, only about five per cent of the Protestants regularly attend church services.

In the early 1900's, the German visitors at a trade-union congress in England were shocked to see the British delegates rise to be led in prayer by one of their number, a free church pastor. To them, a pastor was simply a servant of a church tied to an authoritarian state, with no interest in the workingman. A quarter-century later, German pastors were equally shocked when Clara Zarbach, a churchwoman and social worker, prayed with the members of a socialist trade-union as she helped them organize a strike. No loyal church member would associate with socialists—or strikers!

That estrangement between German church and German workingman symbolized the state of irrelevancy into which the state church had fallen by the first quarter of the twentieth century. It had begun years earlier when the ruling princes of the separate states, later the emperor of a united nation, had functioned also as head of the church. The epithet *Thron und Altar* epitomized the relationship between the world, as represented by the ruling classes, and the church as an institution whose pastors and officials were functionaries of a secular state. That being so, there was no tension between them; by accommodating herself to the expectations of the state, the church rescinded her obligation to speak out in challenge or judgment on government or society. Similarly, she had so sought to accommodate her message to the prevailing concepts of philosophy and political theory that her liberal theology had become indistinguishable from other disciplines. And in the face of rising miseries growing out of ruthless industrialization, she remained comfortably aloof, disdainful of socialistic ferments, secure in her own privileged position as an arm of the state. She had become irrelevant; she had nothing to say that mattered.

True, in the century before World War II individual voices rose to warn against prostitution of the gospel message entrusted to the church. In protest against her accommodation to rationalistic trends, some conservative churchmen had taken refuge in pietistic circles where otherworldly personal concerns were uppermost; others migrated to found rigorously disciplined Lutheran churches in the new world—partly in reaction to the early nineteenth century formation of Lutheran and Reformed bodies alike into regional state churches. Scoring indifference and self-sufficiency, certain reformers—among them Pastors Theodor Fliedner, J. H. Wichern, and Friedrich von Bodelschwingh—won wide response to their calls for church renewal and development of social concern. Out of their efforts grew a number of remarkable charitable institutions: the deaconess service, refuges for the mentally ill and the physically handicapped, the all-embracing Inner Mission enterprise. These, while under the aegis of the church but not organically related to it, have proved lasting channels for the energies of men and women eager to serve others. There were others—Rudolf Todt, Adolph Stöcker, Friedrich Naumann—who called on the church to concern itself with the growing ranks of the proletariat and who, failing to arouse the kind of response they wanted, turned to politics and, in varying degree, to nationalistic nostrums. But in the main, the church as an institution remained content to preserve her privileged status.

The rise of nazism and the debacle that culminated in World War II shocked the German Protestant churches into critical self-evaluation and reassessment of their role in the nation's life. Adolf Hitler's attempt to ally the church with the Nazis' glorification of the German race found some churchmen willing to go along, to accept rigged election to places of ecclesiastical power as "German Christians." But there were many who held back. Some did so out of conviction that the state had no right to interfere in purely ecclesiastical affairs. But a significant minority was appalled to discover what Nazi ideology and practice revealed about the church's historical failure to make her essential message plain and pertinent, and to demonstrate concern for the nation's social and political life. Among them were a number of pastors who had been active in the Student Christian Movement in their university days and who had since been caught up by the resurgence of interest in Reformation studies. In particular, there were some who had been active in the *Berneuchen Kreis,* a circle of youth leaders who, in 1926, in their controversial *Berneuchen Buch,* had bluntly warned that unless the church regained her New Testament nature as a channel for God's love to all men, and overcame her impotence and irrelevance in the face of a rapidly changing society, she was doomed to "die within her own walls."

In January, 1933, a group of these men—along with others who shared their concern—met together and issued a declaration opposing the subservience of the "German Christians." They then formed what they called "pastors' emergency leagues" in the various regional churches. In September of that year some two thousand pastors attending the national synod of the regional churches in Wittenberg went so far as to voice a protest against the new Nazi law barring Christian Jews from congregations. "We must obey God rather than man," they said, and constituted a "confessing church" across regional boundary lines. The next year members of this "church"— free of the restricting bonds of ecclesiastical officialdom—issued their famous "Barmen Declaration" which, when word of it reached other countries, was hailed as a sign that new leaven was at work in the German church. Two statements from that manifesto revealed how far its signers had moved from the assumptions of the established church: "We reject the false doctrine that there are realms of life that do not belong to Jesus Christ, but to other masters, realms that do not need to be justified or sanctified by Him." "We reject the false doctrine that the church should go beyond its special task and assume functions and dignities of the state, thus itself becoming an organ of the state."

There followed a period which has been called the "ghetto years" of the German churches. What began as simple opposition to the "apostasy" of the "German Christians" developed into denial by sensitive churchmen of all in nazism that was destroying the dignity and rights of the individual. Though the movement made little impact on the great body of nominal church members, it did awaken the concern of many of the clergy for the essential import of the gospel message, and it led to a new appreciation of the church as a community through which God's spirit operates, not as a national institution. In regional brotherhoods—actually clandestine cells—clergy and laymen who shared this vision of the church's real nature came together in a new sense of fellowship. Later, many of the pastors who became outspoken in opposition to Nazi practices were imprisoned; some were put to death. From the ranks of these "confessing" churchmen came much of the postwar leadership that has sought to arouse a concern for the people outside the churches' doors as men and women who deserve an opportunity not only to hear but to be heard.

Such a church-world encounter, it soon became clear, was unlikely to come about within the rigid, time-honored form of German parish life, hampered by class consciousness, a pattern in which the congregation had become simply the passive recipient of God's Word as handed down by the pastor in traditional, often obscure terms. And at the end of World War II the German people desperately needed to hear that Word in clear and relevant terms. Defeated, rudderless, disillusioned by the collapse of their "chosen people" dream, suspicious of all ideologies after their experience with nazism, those who were not simply abjectly apathetic were grasping for some meaning in life, some chance for community living, some indication that they might hope for more in life than being manipulated by blind force.

BAD BOLL

It was in this situation that the movement exemplified by today's German Evangelical academies got its start. It might even be traced back to a discussion between two men, who had been active in the "confessing church," during a chance meeting at Tübingen just at the time the Allied advance was bringing the Nazis' world down about their ears. Helmut Thielicke, who had been driven from his theological professorship at the University of Tübingen by the Nazis, and Eberhard Müller, former student pastor and army chaplain, were convinced that the spiritual catastrophe of nazism stemmed, in part, from the fact that the church's message had ceased to influence the nation's social and political life noticeably, and had become irrelevant to the workaday lives of its nominal members who simply paid it no mind. What was needed, the young men concluded, was radical experimentation to discover a new form of encounter between church and world which would challenge men's interest, make the church aware of the problems that cry out for solution, and bridge the gap of indifference between the church and the great body of her laity. No longer was the old parish system, established when people lived and worked in a self-sufficient, isolated rural milieu, adequate to meet the needs of a people flung by industrialization far out from the comfortable boundaries of home and village. No longer could the mere academic discussion of biblical texts and the authoritarian answers to skeptical questionings suffice for people beset by wracking problems demanding pragmatic solutions.

Thielicke and Müller conceived the idea of an "academy"—a place where people from the isolated social and vocational circles of German society might come together on neutral ground in common search for answers to baffling everyday problems. And it just might be that the churchmen who provided the neutral ground would gain new insights themselves into theological suppositions, and direct that insight to illuminate the dilemmas faced by "post-Christian" man. One requirement, they were sure, must be observed: the theologians who served as hosts must not dictate; communication must be free, open, and tolerant.

Looking about for a place to implement these plans, Müller met a Moravian bishop who told him that the American military authorities were allowing re-establishment of his church's headquarters, moved from Herrnhut in the face of the Russian advance, in the health resort village of Bad Boll, fifty miles southeast of Stuttgart. The four hundred rooms of the resort hotel would not be used, and the bishop offered them for the use of the proposed academy.

A favorable site thus available, Müller and Thielicke enlisted the aid of Bishop Theophil Wurm of the regional Church of Württemberg, in which Bad Boll lies. Bishop Wurm at that time was the most prominent churchman in Germany; his sturdy reaction to Hitler's attempt to prostitute the church for his own ends gave him prestige in those early postwar days. He himself sent out invitations to the first academy session—on "Justice in Social and Political Life." Since there were no postal and public transportation facilities in that summer of 1945, messengers on motorcycle delivered invitations to the industrialists and lawyers for whom the first conference was designed. To the organizers' pleased surprise, one hundred fifty men turned up at Bad Boll for the sessions. For two weeks, beginning September 29 (the day of St. Michael, who has since become the unofficial patron saint of the lay movement), representatives of these two vocational groups with heavy responsibilities for rebuilding the nation wrestled with problems of justice. To the pleased surprise of the laymen, the theologians did not silence their arguments with dogmatic replies but listened attentively and engaged in sympathetic and constructive analysis.

Inspired by their experience, buoyed up by the opportunity for free expression and honest search which had been denied them for years, the participants in that first conference spread enthusiastic word of the new venture at Bad Boll. There were requests from all sides that the experiment be continued. So, satisfied that a small bridgehead had been established on the secular side of the gulf, the planners turned their attention to the opposite bank. They arranged a conference for church administrators to discuss ecclesiastical bureaucracy and to learn about the venture at Bad Boll. In December, a conference for factory workers taught Thielicke and Müller and their co-workers a lesson in procedure. Because invitations went out through parish pastors, the only workers who turned up were already committed Christians active in parish life, entirely unrepresentative of the great mass of laboring people. Fortunately, the lesson came early. Two years later, when a second factory workers' conference was attempted, the invitations were extended through union and management channels, and a representative cross section of workers accepted. The sessions were extremely productive; in recent years, Bad Boll's work with laboring men and women has become one of its most extensive and successful features.

During its second year of operation the academy sponsored twenty-five conferences, mainly for members of specific vocational groups: farmers, physicians, civil servants, journalists. By 1947, the number had grown to one hundred thirty. A pattern of daily procedure, established at the first conference, continued: opening worship in which participation was voluntary; Bible study on a specific theme; presentation of the main topic by experts in the field; open discussion; evening worship, again voluntary; opportunity throughout for informal conversation, coffee breaks, and recreation.

Among those who particularly welcomed the opportunity to go to Bad Boll in its early days were men penalized in the denazification process: teachers and civil servants, for instance, who had served under the prewar regime and now were banned by the authorities from resuming their occupations. During the first two years, ten conferences for teachers and school officials from all over the state of Württemberg were attended by fifteen hundred men and women. Conference leaders were gratified to note how eagerly the teachers, free from the need to trim their sails to the latest ideological shift, tackled such problems as the overcoming of the Nazi mentality, the difference between humanist and Christian views of education, and so on. And they had reason to hope that the deliberations at Bad Boll helped the teachers adjust to life in postwar Germany. A special conference for journalists at Bad Boll—just a year after the academy opened—attracted wide notice, as might have been expected. Not so expected was the comprehensive and perceptive nature of the news coverage. Since then the themes developed at annual conferences for journalists have continued to be widely featured in the secular press and the conclusions reached have had a beneficial influence on public attitudes.

ARNOLDSHAIN

Because of the lack of regular means of communication in Germany at the time of its inception, word of the experiment at Bad Boll did not spread at once beyond Württemberg. So it cannot be determined just how much influence the first academy had on others established at about the same time. Problems crying for attention beset the regional churches, and everywhere men were searching for some way to deal with them; it is not surprising that ventures similar to Bad Boll appeared within the next few years.

The Church of Hessen-Nassau, centering on Frankfort on the Main and now headed by Martin Niemöller, was not formally organized in its present form until late in 1946. By then it already had an academy in fact, if not in name, in the series of retreats inaugurated the previous December by church men's work leaders, which were being held at a resort hotel near Bad Nauheim. Later this program developed into the flourishing Evangelical academy with its own beautiful modern building crowning a wooded slope above the village of Arnoldshain, in the Taunus mountains north of Frankfort. Only eight people came to the first vocational conference (for teachers) organized by the Hessen-Nassau academy, but by the end of its first year of operation one thousand men and women had taken part in the ten conferences offered: five for teachers, three for lawyers, two for physicians. In one significant early series of meetings, parents, teachers, and pastors gave earnest study to a critical problem of the day: What was to be Germany's future attitude toward the Jews? In 1948, the academy initiated "problem conferences" on specific economic and political issues.

Though, unlike Bad Boll, it grew out of an official church activity, the Arnoldshain academy has developed as independently as those which began without sponsorship by ecclesiastical organizations.

LOCCUM

Following the lead of Bad Boll as a separate center, an academy was established within the domain of the Church of Hannover. It got its start in Hermannsburg, a town which, for many years, had been a center of missionary training. After the war a group of university graduates in Hermannsburg who shared a hope for renewal in the church decided to come together in bi-weekly meetings to discuss their responsibilities in rebuilding the shattered German nation. Spurred by the results of their conversations and fellowship, they considered the possibility of bringing in others by establishing some sort of discussion center. A team of Allied soldiers moved out of a partially bombed hotel in the town, which they had used while "mopping up" munition caches; the churchmen put an "occupied" sign on the door and had their center. But funds and official support were lacking. Early in 1946 the group commissioned Johannes Doehring, a former army chaplain who had addressed one of their meetings, to solicit such support from Hanns Lilje, just elected bishop of the regional Church of Hannover in the reorganization that followed the Nazi downfall and the eclipse of the "German Christians."

In his student days and later, Hanns Lilje had been active in leadership of the Student Christian Movement—in Germany and internationally—and he had been a prime mover in the "confessing church." Courageously vocal in opposition to the Nazi regime, he had finally been imprisoned. After a series of trials he was sentenced to death; the arrival of an advanced Allied unit at the prison, on the day set for his execution, saved his life. He had observed the degradation that blind fidelity to an ungodly ideology wrought in the personalities of his captors; he became convinced that some new way must be found to relate the Christian gospel to men's lives. Immediately after becoming bishop, he began to organize teams of laymen and pastors who shared his concern. They carried their message into factories, schools, and streets; then conducted community rallies.

Hanns Lilje's response to Doehring's plea was spontaneous; he realized that what the group at Hermannsburg envisaged embodied an idea that had been germinating in the "confessing church." And the Church of Hannover, like all the regional churches, did have funds on hand, accumulated from the church tax. Grants from those funds, plus gifts from interested churchmen, made possible the opening of the Hermannsburg center on a permanent basis in September, 1946. In the very first conference, a link with Bad Boll was evident; one of the lecturers was Helmut Thielicke. As at Bad Boll, the invitations to the first event were sent out by the bishop of the regional church and Lilje himself gave one of the lectures. By the end of 1946, seven conferences had brought some three hundred men and women to Hermannsburg; during the next year there were twenty conferences and around fifteen hundred participants.

In the introduction to the booklet, *Signs of Renewal,* the report on the European lay centers by the World Council of Churches' Department on the Laity, Kathleen Bliss (see page 30) writes of the early days of the Hermannsburg academy: "In October 1946 I paid a visit to Germany. Post-war conditions were still severe: cities were in ruins and thousands of people were living in cellars; food was scarce and poor; travel was difficult; Germany was an occupied country under military rule. In these inauspicious conditions the Evangelical academies were beginning to do the work which has now rightly made them famous. I travelled over bomb-shattered roads to the village of Hermannsburg, some distance from Hannover. Here, in conditions of stark simplicity, eating black bread and potato soup, a group of journalists and former editors of German newspapers were discussing the future of the press in Germany. They discussed not in academic generalizations but with a sense of practical urgency. Germany had had no free press for years: even now military censorship was severe, but the conditions were beginning to favor the emergence of responsible German journalism, and soon freedom would return. It did not seem a moment too soon to discuss why that freedom had been lost and what use was to be made of it when it returned. The Evangelical Academy was providing both the place for such a discussion, an oasis of peace in turbulence, and the staff, theologically trained and freed from other responsibilities in order to devote themselves to the work."[1]

In the years since 1946, annual successors to that first journalists' conference which so impressed Mrs. Bliss have contributed greatly toward more responsible and comprehensive handling of public issues by the long-stifled German press. The conferences draw leaders in the field of journalism from all over West Germany, and reports of the discussions in the secular newspapers acquaint the general public with the issues. In the planning stage and in actual execution, these conferences receive the personal attention of Bishop Lilje, a journalist himself as editor of *Sonntagsblatt,* a weekly newspaper devoted to all facets of modern culture which reveals only in basic viewpoint that it is church-related. Among the themes with which the annual conferences have dealt are "The Modern Crisis of Man," "The Depreciation of Words," "Responsibility Before God," "New Powers Governing Society," and "The Phenomenon of Nazism."

In 1952, the Hermannsburg academy moved to beautiful new quarters—a handsome building, contemporary in design and furnishing—just outside the pleasant village of Loccum, some fifty miles northwest of Hannover. In authorizing the move, the Church of Hannover no doubt intended to link new life to the church's ancient roots. For across a tree-shaded vale from the spreading center stands the twelfth-century abbey of Loccum, where monks and brothers once studied and labored and which now is the property

[1] Hans-Ruedi Weber, ed., *Signs of Renewal* (Geneva: World Council of Churches, Department on the Laity, 1957), pp. 4-5.

of the church. To the sturdy, worn-stone abbey, with its priceless library of volumes new and old (some of the latter bound in ancient vellum), come selected seminarians, after three years of theoretical theological study, for an additional year of practical study and work. They may participate in the academy program, and academy conferees are welcome at the Sunday worship services conducted by the parish pastor in the abbey's high-walled chapel. From time to time committees and other official units of the Church of Hannover come to the abbey for their meetings, and when occasion demands Bishop Lilje is on hand to preside as Abbot John XII of Loccum.

Recalling Hermannsburg's missionary tradition, many lay people invited to conferences in the early years hesitated to accept, suspecting a proselyting motive behind the offer of a neutral meeting place. But would-be critics were disarmed by the academy's methods: frank and honest discussion without restrictions, sympathetic consideration of opposite views, and the attempt to reconcile rather than coerce. As at Bad Boll, the proceedings at Loccum are set in a framework of Bible study and corporate worship in which participation is voluntary. Though many of the people who attend the conferences have never attended worship services, many find themselves doing so before the sessions are over.

The Loccum building is spacious and comfortable, with conference rooms, assembly halls, an adequate library, a chapel with contemporary decor, private bedrooms, dining halls, lounge, and a broad terrace where guests gather for coffee and wine breaks in fine weather. On the grounds are separate residences for the staff. Pastor Doehring is co-director of the center, with Hans Bolewski.

To a greater extent than many of the other academies, Loccum has made a conscious effort to set up conferences for people in places of responsibility in the new Germany. Particularly effective have been those arranged for national leaders in industry, on such themes as "Human Relations in Industry," "Men and Machines," "Marxism," "Prices and Wages," "Bureaucracy," and "The Ethical

Basis of Politics." This last conference was attended by Chancellor Konrad Adenauer, among others.

In still another type of conference, Loccum brings together representatives of vocational groups between which there is likely to be tension—editors and reporters, nurses and physicians, industrial managers and workers—and gives them an opportunity to talk out their differences face to face. Usually some degree of reconciliation ensues. At other conferences, pastors and lay church workers discuss their problems and, the academy hopes, gain new perspective on their tasks and an awareness of the human needs that often lie about them unnoticed.

Though Loccum has laid less stress than some of the other academies on programs designed especially for industrial workers, it has had successes in that field. Its first conference for factory workers enrolled over one hundred men. In 1953, it initiated a "young workers' conference" in which employers cooperate by giving apprentices leave to attend fourteen-day sessions at the academy. The young men attend lectures and meet for discussion in what amounts to a miniature liberal arts course, and take part in a round of recreational activities. Voluntary worship services are conducted at the beginning and close of each day. As a rule, at least two-thirds of the apprentices are frankly anti-Christian or indifferent to religion. "What are they trying to get out of us?" they usually ask at first, particularly when they discover that their employers are paying their expenses. "What can the church have to say to *us?*" More often than not, however, they leave impressed; and the next contingent is likely to include young people who have heard their predecessors' recommendations and warnings that they will be missing something new and worthwhile if they refuse to go.

Of lasting importance have been Loccum's conferences for young refugees from East Germany and other regions now under Communist control. For many of them, it is the first chance they have ever had to discuss social, political, or religious questions in an atmosphere of complete freedom; to voice frustrations and dissatisfactions which might otherwise lead to bitterness and revolt. On the staff is one social worker who devotes her entire time to the problems of refugee families. She pays regular visits to the large refugee camp nearby, one of several regional centers where newcomers from the East live until permanent work and homes are found for them. Earlier, an important function of the academy was to help ease tensions between newly-arrived refugees and the communities compelled to serve as their hosts; but with the reduction of job and housing shortages the need for this type of reconciliation has become less acute. As 1960 opened, Loccum could report that, in thirteen years of operation, it had been host to over fifty-five thousand people at its conferences and workshops.

There are now eighteen Evangelical academies in Germany, including four in the Soviet zone. On an average, they sponsor about six hundred conferences a year, with a total attendance of around forty-eight thousand. Though they are affiiliated with the official state churches (Lutheran, Reformed, and Union), the minority free churches have been represented on many of the academy boards, and everyone is welcome to participate in the conferences.

HAMBURG

Some of the academies, like the three earliest at Bad Boll, Arnoldshain, and Loccum, are housed in their own specially equipped buildings. Others have no permanent quarters. Among the latter is the academy of the Church of Hamburg, whose special nature is determined in part by its existence in the one regional German church which is entirely urban. It sponsors evening lecture series, many of them held at the University of Hamburg, which draw audiences of one hundred or more. Typical of the topics dealt with are: "Medicine and Theology," "The Church and Contemporary Social Problems," "Reason and Revelation," and "The Christian Statesman." In addition, the Hamburg academy sponsors study circles among vocational groups, with experts from the pertinent field leading each discussion. From time to time it also conducts retreats for churchmen at one or another of the local vacation resorts. Tentative plans have been made for erection of a permanent academy building in a rural setting north of the city which would serve both the Church of Hamburg and the Church of Schleswig-Holstein in their lay endeavors; however, no definite commitments have been made.

SCHLESWIG-HOLSTEIN

The Schleswig-Holstein academy operates much like the one in Hamburg, sponsoring lectures and conferences at various places: the student center at the University of Kiel, the cathedral hall in Ratzeburg, and elsewhere. Since 1953, it has occasionally had the use of a provincial education center near the Danish border. This academy was initiated by former Student Christian Movement members and laymen who were active in the program of Hilfswerk, the postwar relief agency of the German Protestant churches. It continues to give prominent place to student meetings and conferences. From the start it enjoyed the enthusiastic support of the bishop of the regional church; at present, the chairman of its board is a member of the theological faculty at the University of Kiel.

A special feature of the Schleswig-Holstein academy is a number of lay conferences designed to revive, within existing congregations, the office of deacon; and to develop an informed and responsible body of lay men and women who will exert a Christian influence in their daily work and so help bring an end to the era of the "pastors' church." In these four-day conferences, daytime courses are offered which in some ways resemble the leadership training sessions conducted by American churches, but which lay greater emphasis on underlying doctrine. The evenings are given over to lectures.

At the same time, the Schleswig-Holstein academy, like its fellows, carries on a program throughout the year of two- to six-day conferences arranged for people within various social and occupational groupings. In the year beginning July 1, 1958, twenty-six such conferences were offered throughout the state. A partial listing of the groups which participated indicates their variety: midwives; dancing teachers and church youth; tenant farmers and freeholders; pedagogical and theological students; police officers; foreign students, actors, and journalists; Freemasons and church officers; Christians and freethinkers (their topic: "Christian and Materialistic Messiah-ship"); army officers and teachers from the Danish boundary zone; industrial workers and managers; pensioners and people nearing retirement; Lutheran and Roman Catholic theologians (on "The Second Sacrament"); Orthodox and Lutheran students (on "Martyrdom").

BERLIN AND EAST ZONE

The Evangelical academy in Berlin operates much like those in Hamburg and Schleswig-Holstein, sponsoring lectures and discussion groups in both East and West zones and serving, so far as it is able, as a meeting place for churchmen within each area and across the separating line between them.

Four other lay centers in the Soviet zone continue to carry on courageously, if circumspectly. There churchmen can meet and discuss problems of parish and family life. First to be established was the Evangelical academy of Saxony-Anhalt, which maintains an office at the cathedral in Magdeburg but holds many of its meetings in the Luther Hall at Wittenberg and elsewhere. Usually, the topics chosen explore school, job, and community interests; sometimes science and theology. Though this academy necessarily cannot offer formal discussions on political issues, it does occasionally bring together people who represent opposing ideologies and encourages frank exchange of opinion. The results, in a land where such exchange is seldom possible, have been salutary; and since everything is perfectly open and aboveboard, the academy has not become a special object of suspicion.

Topics are chosen with discrimination, too, at the academy of the Church of Saxony, at Meissen, not far from Dresden and the Czech border. A castle belonging to the local cathedral houses the program and provides living quarters for the cathedral dean, who is also director of studies for the academy. In spite of many handicaps, the academy at Meissen manages to carry on a lively and warmly welcomed program; in 1959 it was host to no fewer than forty-five conferences covering religious, social, and cultural subjects. With so many religious activities curtailed in the Soviet zone, the pastors and loyal church workers meeting at Meissen with people from other parishes find encouraging assurance that the church is a living body capable of fruitful life regardless of the society in which it exists. The two other Soviet zone academies are at Jena, in the area of the Church of Thuringia, and at Güstrow, in the lake region of northern Mecklenburg.

TUTZING

Perhaps because its beautiful lakeside castle home (Tutzing) lies in the vicinity of a colony of artists, philosophers, and writers who have been attracted to the alpine setting, the Evangelical academy of the Church of Bavaria has given special attention to the arts, though it has by no means neglected other areas of German life. One Tutzing conference which attracted wide attention, in the press and elsewhere, brought jazz musicians and pastors together to explore the significance of rhythm in life. Famous German jazz bands played, and there was lively discussion on such topics as "The Tempo of Life as a Theological Problem" and "Jazz: Its Biological and Cosmological Origins"—a range of investigation which must have led to "way out" conclusions but which surely could not be charged with being humdrum. Another off-beat encounter had as its theme "Fashion," with models and designers delving into the implications of their profession in German life and the motivation lying behind their work.

Not all Tutzing's conferences are off-beat. Deliberately trying to avoid a mass approach, this academy has set up many small, intensive discussions among members of a wide range of occupations. For instance, physicians, pharmacists, representatives of pharmaceutical firms, and government officials have met to consider the use and misuse of drugs; secretaries have tried to analyze the problems of the career woman in the midst of a man's world; war widows have shared the troubles they have trying to bring up a family without a father and without adequate income; refugees from the East have sought help as they try to adjust to being a not-too-welcome minority in West Germany. On several occasions—again the off-beat—conferences have brought to Tutzing skilled and unskilled workers to discuss, not wage problems or labor relations, but the literary works of authors all the way from Sophocles to Stalin and Thornton Wilder! Once, unmarried mothers were invited to come to the academy for an objective look at their situation in German society; again, pastors and members of their congregations met to debate—of all things—"The Sermon."

Tutzing was initiated by Bishop Hans Meiser, and has always been closely related to the Church of Bavaria. Like the other academies, it is host to church conferences, and its charming site on the shore of Starnberger Lake makes it a favorite place for summer meetings of church representatives from all over Germany. In August, 1959, for instance, a commission set up in 1956 by the Evangelical Church in Germany—the postwar federation of official Lutheran, Reformed, and Union regional churches—met there to study the history of the church's struggle in the Nazi period. The commission is charged with collecting, appraising, and publishing original material on the conflict with Hitler, before such information is irretrievably lost. Such a service, it is agreed, will prove increasingly valuable as the memory of what happened during those days fades, and the danger arises that revival of the spirit which imbued the Nazi movement may again win a hearing. Few efforts are being made in Germany today to preserve a record of the excesses of the Nazi period, and it is to the credit of the Protestant churches that they are concerned for such a project. A significant collection has been made in Bielefeld, at the church of which Wilhelm Niemöller, brother of Martin, is pastor.

HAUS VILLIGST

Another collection exists at Haus Villigst, not an academy but a remarkable church social institution in the Ruhr valley, which carries on a productive program of research and experiment designed to make the church aware of the problems of industrial workers and miners in the area. Under the aegis of the Church of Westphalia, seminars bring workers and foremen from surrounding plants to discuss common problems under the direction of the staff sociologists and theologians. Apprentices live in the rambling old mansion which houses the project, carrying on a program of studies after their day's work is over. University students spend six-month terms at the house while they earn money in industry to carry on their education; in the process, they experience and study the problems of working men. As to the "remember nazism" venture, the young history professor on the staff explains, "Somehow no one wants to think about it, and the schools avoid the subject. But here we have primary sources—letters, documents, eyewitness accounts—and we discuss the sorry period thoroughly, as it must be if the same sort of thing is not to happen again."

HAUS DER BEGEGNUNG

Conferences for men who work in the mines and factories of the lower Ruhr area are emphasized, also, at Haus der Begegnung (House of Encounter), a lay academy which serves the churches of the Rhineland and Westphalia. Housed in a comfortable old mansion in a wooded park near Mülheim, not far from the confluence of the Ruhr and Rhine rivers, it has accommodations for sixty. It does not confine its offerings to men on the assembly line; one of its earliest conferences, for chemists and engineers, was built around the question "Is Technology the Hope of the World?" In

1953, the first year of its operation, Haus der Begegnung was host to over fifty conferences, with almost three thousand participants. The schedule for only the last four months in 1959 listed forty two- or three-day conferences. There is an amazing variety of topics, among them: "Communism as a Challenge to Christianity," "Must Capital Punishment Be Continued?" (for jurists), "Man in Industry" (a continuing series, with sessions at stated intervals), "The Abnormality of Man's Situation," "The Literary Work of Albert Camus" (for teachers and students of literature, booksellers, and librarians), "Church-State-Vocation" (likewise a continuing series), "A Meeting with Picasso" (analysis and interpretation), "Preparation for Retirement," "The Ethics of the Soldier" (for young military officers and pastors), and "Wherein Lies Political and Economic Freedom in the West?"

Regularly, Haus der Begegnung is host also to "outside" groups: meetings sponsored by the sociology and ethics department of the Church of the Rhineland, conferences arranged by leaders in the mining industry, seminars set up by government officials at Bonn, and so on. A somewhat similar program, but on a smaller scale, is carried on in another academy related to the churches of the Rhineland and Westphalia. It is known as Haus Ortlohn.

FRIEDEWALD

An academy on the outskirts of the Rhineland-Westphalia industrial area is related to no particular territorial church, but concerns itself with industry-labor problems all over Germany. Known as the Evangelical Social Academy Friedewald, it is located in a quiet park near Betzdorf. In a way, it continues the training of young labor-union members begun by the school of the Free Church Social Conference, an agency developed in the early 1900's under the leadership of Reinhold Seeberg. Conducted at Berlin-Spandau, it was forced to close down early in the Nazi regime. Friedewald offers three types of training: three-month courses for promising young industrial workers in which basic training in political science, sociology, labor legislation, church history, and public speaking is supplemented by lively discussion of current issues, all designed to overcome ethical indifference of workingmen and to help them develop responsible attitudes toward their jobs and society; six-month courses for men and women preparing to become specialists in social ethics on church staffs; regular academy-type conferences for pastors, students, employers, white collar workers, and industrial employees. Throughout West Germany today, "cells in industry" made up of alumni of the Friedewald training courses are spreading the gospel of ethical responsibility in daily work.

OTHER ACADEMIES

As can be seen from the above descriptions of the work carried on by a number of academies, each has a unique character—a special emphasis—though all share similar purposes and operate with similar methods.

The union Church of Baden's academy, at Herrenalb in the Black Forest, has been termed the "most European" of the lot because of its greater (though not exclusive) concern with theoretical theology. Perhaps typical of its offerings are these, noted at random: "Protestantism and Europe," "The Power of Silence," "Predestination and Freedom," "Modern Man and the Sacraments." Herrenalb was established in 1947, and at first was located in Falkenburg.

A new building was recently completed for the academy of the United Protestant Church of the Palatinate (Pfalz), which covers an area near the French border in which the majority of the people are Roman Catholic. Standing on a gentle rise in wooded hill country near Bad Dürkheim, the center offers pleasant surroundings for conferences. A wing spreading from the main building is used by young people who hike or cycle to the academy for meetings and for picnics at tables provided for them in an arched passageway. This union church, in which Reformed elements predominate, has in recent years established fellowship with Congregational churches in other countries. One of the functions of the academy is to foster mutual encouragement among people who are a minority in their environment. The academy of the Church of Kurhessen-Waldeck, another union body, was begun in 1947 as the result of the interest of churchmen who had been impressed by the lectures and discussion at the Hessen-Nassau academy when it was still in temporary quarters near Bad Nauheim. Located at Hofgeismar, it has had notable success in gathering people from all occupations and all levels of society to consider man's situation in the world today and the forces that have alienated him from roots that give security and initiative. The academy of the Church of Oldenburg maintains its office in the city of Oldenburg but sponsors some of its conferences at a resort hotel on the North Sea. It holds frequent week-end meetings for members of different professional groups, and has provided a number of seminar-type conferences for industrial workers.

ONE ACADEMY'S ACTIVITIES

In 1952, the earliest of the German Evangelical academies moved from the Bad Boll resort hotel to its own beautiful, comfortable quarters on a tree-bordered slope some four hundred yards away, across a winding, quiet stream. The main lodge, in contemporary style, has rooms especially designed for conferences and informal conversation, libraries, recreation rooms, and dormitory and dining space for the hundreds who participate in the academy programs. Adjoining the main building, a renovated "castle" offers additional space for offices and informal conference sessions. A chapel is central to the plan. Nearby are residences to accommodate many of the permanent staff, which now numbers over eighty; of these, two-thirds are theologians or professional directors, the rest service employees.

Thus equipped, Bad Boll is able to conduct several conferences simultaneously. In the course of one month it may be host to as many as twenty, made up of men and women of whom an estimated ninety per cent have previously been completely indifferent to the church, some vocally hostile to its claims. There are few distractions in the neighborhood of the academy, set in the midst of a gently rolling countryside whose meticulously tended farm strips center on tiny old-fashioned villages from which men and women go out daily to till the fields or, increasingly, to join the throngs commuting to jobs at the great industrial establishments in the valley between Bad Boll and Stuttgart.

From time to time, in the academy's conference rooms, groups of farmers may be found debating the ethics involved in the proposed reassignment of the bits of privately owned farmland whose lack of contiguity has long made tilling the soil a wasteful and toilsome business in this part of Germany. Or students from the technical high schools may be considering the place of the individual in a mechanistic age; teachers, their responsibility to train children to be responsible participants in a democratic society; trade-union members, the implications of automation; women factory workers, the rival claims of family and job; mayors of villages and towns, the temptations of bureaucracy; artists, the significance of modern design—and so on through the whole range of modern vocations and cultural interests.

As at the other Evangelical academies, the immediate aim at Bad Boll is not to convert participants to Christianity or to expound the Christian viewpoint against all challenges, but to spur exchange of opinion in a friendly, neutral atmosphere—between right and left; between the tradition-bound and the emancipated; above all, between the church and the estranged. The result is honest probing for workable solutions, therapeutic reconciling of differences, stimulation of respect between men. Throughout all this, however, there is a pervasive religious aura, neither self-consciously inserted nor compulsory. A period of Bible study pertinent to the themes under discussion follows breakfast each day, and morning and evening worship services are held in the chapel. Many conferees unaccustomed to formal worship or Bible study are found to be taking part before the conference period is over. On hand at all times are the theologians on the staff, ready for consultation as the discussion proceeds and as little groups gather in the wide-windowed lounges for informal conversation and refreshments.

The leadership at each Bad Boll conference is made up of experts in the field under discussion, along with those staff members who are best equipped to cope with the chosen theme. These staff members are engaged in preparation for their conferences from the moment they are scheduled. I learned about the typical preliminary preparation when I went to Bad Boll to visit the Y.W.C.A. secretary (a graduate economist) whose primary responsibility is the academy's work with women in industry. She had just returned from the first in a series of planning sessions for a conference of department store clerks, still a couple of months away.

"Yesterday I met at luncheon in a Stuttgart restaurant with others on the planning team—a sociologist and a theologian from the staff here, a union officer and a store manager," she said. "We spent two hours talking about what are the most difficult problems department store clerks face in these high cost, high pressure, competitive times; deciding which would recommend themselves as the most productive topics for exploration in the light of Christian principles. Then we considered which experts we would invite to serve as leaders—to introduce the themes and lead the discussions. That was just laying the groundwork. Now we'll get busy determining what final form the topics will take, what in the discussion is likely to pose the greatest challenge to our leaders' talents of exposition and reconciliation. Finally, we will send out announcements to clerks in stores whose managers have shown enough interest in our program to supply us with names from their rosters, or whose union leaders have been willing to join in our plans. Meanwhile, we will be at work moving along preparations for other conferences, and carrying out those scheduled for these weeks.

Preparation and execution march along together, like trains on parallel tracks, with one trailing behind the other."

I saw some of the typical announcements sent out for this and other conferences. They are beautifully designed and laid out, their motifs imaginatively reflecting the theme to be considered, or making use of the arch symbol which conveys what the academy hopes to be—a bridge between church and world. The texts are concise, intriguingly worded, set in attractive type faces on wide-margined pages. If the clerks' response ran true to form, applications to attend that department store clerks' conference outnumbered even Bad Boll's spacious facilities.

Conferences such as this make up only one phase of a program that keeps the Bad Boll staff constantly busy. All up and down the teeming valley leading to Stuttgart, and in the city itself, certain staff members are busy carrying out the academy's extension program. "Labor pastors," working under a special office created within the Church of Württemburg, cooperate in some phases of this work. The program operates through cell groups of conference alumni in the textile, machine tool, metal work, and other plants; through evening meetings in workers' homes; and through occasional "Workers' Weeks." These weeks include daytime discussion meetings for families, evening rallies centering around some current economic or social issue, an informal Saturday evening banquet attended by representatives of labor, management, and the church, plus a final Sunday worship service and a summary of the week's deliberations.

At all these peripheral Bad Boll conferences-in-miniature, skilled staff members from the academy act as advisers; ready to listen, to clarify and, when occasion arises, to relate issues raised to basic Christian principles. Ideally, wondering and perplexed men and women could find such services in the parish church. But it has been long since Germany's workers have looked to the church for aid in everyday matters. And even if pastoral concern were present there, the parishes are so huge and understaffed, and the shift of daily life's focus from home community to distant place of employment so pronounced, that the ideal is seldom realized. Meanwhile, Bad Boll's cells in industry and its house circles provide an opening wedge; while persistent efforts are made, both by the academy and by the official regional church, to arouse parish pastors' interest in adopting new methods of contact with the workers, to involve pastors in discussions set up especially for them at the academy, and to encourage them to attend—under a rule of silence—the various conferences for occupational groups held there.

THE ACADEMIES' ROLE

How, eventually, can all the new interest aroused by the Evangelical academies be channeled into the ongoing stream of German church life? That question is being pondered by leaders of all the lay centers, both those which enjoy close and sympathetic ties with regional church authorities and those which, in the face of official indifference or mistrust, are obliged to carry on more or less independently. Now that initial successes justifying the original thrust have been achieved, leaders are giving special attention to that perplexing question. They recognize the real danger that industrial workers in particular, for so long resentful toward the state church as a bourgeois symbol, may come to look on the academy and its program as a satisfactory substitute for the church. And not just the industrial workers, as I discovered when I sat in on a week-end conference at the Hessen-Nassau academy at Arnoldshain, part of a series on fundamentals of the Christian faith. The conferences had been spurred by a staff member's discovery that a number of professional people in the Frankfurt area not active in the church were asking questions about the bearing certain biblical precepts might have on today's perplexities. A cross section of teachers, physicians, housewives, businessmen and technicians within a fifty-mile radius of the center had been invited to attend discussions set up to explore these questions. More applications had come in than could be accepted, since Arnoldshain can accommodate only about seventy guests. Under the codirector, Heinrich Renkewitz, a Moravian minister who by special dispensation serves also as relief pastor of the local parish church, the participants in the session held that September week end were seeking to discover the relevance of the Bible to the subject of freedom. The answers were not easily come by, as had been the case in earlier sessions on the Ten Commandments. All the guests were enthusiastic about the series yet, Dr. Renkewitz told me, few could be expected to pursue their new-found interest in basic religious concepts to the extent of making contact with churches in their home parishes.

"It is for such people that the lay academies exist," he said. "They are like the majority of Germans today: ready to be interested in a faith that has bearing on their daily lives, but not in the church as the traditional institution they see in their parishes. They are secular, really; church members, yes, but in name only. We are trying to find a new way into people's lives, trying to make our message relevant to what goes on during weekdays. We have to look beyond the all-embracing parish, which is no longer the primary center of people's interest as it was in a more rural, leisurely past. That focus has come to lie elsewhere—in the place where people work, perhaps, or in their union or political party or professional group. Besides, under our parish system many pastors are so taxed with performing the purely mechanical tasks expected of them—like keeping the official records of births, marriages and deaths for all the people, often thousands, who are on their parish rolls as nominal church members—that they have little time to give to purely personal concerns even if they are inclined to do so. Certainly they have little opportunity to become acquainted with the new situations outside their doors that in today's world are making people's lives far different from what they were a couple of generations ago. Most pastors simply follow the line of least resistance—take care of the routine tasks, keep the records up to date, go on preaching the dogmatic expository sermon of yesterday—and try not to notice the growing number of empty pews."

Dr. Renkewitz exemplified the pragmatic approach and, at the same time, the growing hope of all the academy leaders when he concluded, "As we try to introduce the gospel message into the lives of people not used to thinking about it, we realize that they may or may not, probably will not, go to church the next Sunday. But their new concept of what the *meat* of that message is will affect what they do and what they think in the days ahead. Perhaps this is how the missionary task is to be fulfilled in our time right here in Germany. Certainly it is not the traditional, the conventional, way. But who is to say that any one way is *the* way, given the conditions under which modern man lives and labors? Certainly it is no good just trying to 'get people into church.' What has to be done is to get the gospel into people's lives, help them to *be* Christian. If we can do that, perhaps the seeds of renewal will begin to flourish throughout the whole church. We certainly have no intention of establishing a rival 'church'; the enthusiasm with which most of the regional church authorities greet our efforts which, in many cases, they helped launch, testifies against such a charge. It is true that in times past, when efforts were made to spark renewal, new denominations often resulted. Today the trend is toward more, not less, unity. This is the ecumenical age of the church, and since it is on the Christian *message,* not on ecclesiastical doctrine, that the academies lay their emphasis, they are as vital a force for ecumenicity as you will find in Germany today."

Although the procedure of academy programs moves from specific problem to general theory—a new departure from German method—study and research are not neglected. The academies unite to maintain, at Bad Boll, a study center where the results of research from earlier joint plenary sessions and commission meetings are analyzed and compiled for future reference. Some one hundred fifty university professors cooperate in this venture, which covers such areas as theology, education, Marxism, anthropology, and sociology. Many of the topics chosen for investigation within those disciplines grow out of questions raised at academy conferences; they are then referred to a committee which passes them on to selected experts for study.

At Bad Boll, also, are the headquarters of the Directors' Association of the Laymen's Colleges of Europe, as well as the central office of the Directors' Association of the Protestant Academies in Germany. The German directors meet at Bad Boll semiannually, for several days, to discuss common problems and strategies. Their joint office handles certain financial affairs. For instance, it distributes proportonately to the various centers the annual state subsidy that comes out of funds designated for adult education. This subsidy amounts to about twenty-two per cent of each academy's annual budget. Sources of the remainder of budget funds vary from academy to academy. At Bad Boll, for instance, twenty-five per cent comes from Church of Württemberg grants, twenty-two per cent from fees paid by conference participants, seventeen per cent from gifts proffered by "friends of the academy," seven per cent from a private foundation interested in the furtherance of democracy in Germany, and seven per cent from grants made by semigovernmental agencies. Most of the new buildings were erected with funds from the regional churches and personal gifts. Some of the "friends" are individuals or churches in North America. Addressing a laymen's group in New York not long ago, Director Eberhard Müller of the Bad Boll academy declared that without American support during the early years that particular center could not have survived.

Three "floating academies" have grown out of the joint efforts of leaders in the movement throughout Germany. They enjoy support also from certain regional church agencies and from the free churches (which, altogether, have about 500,000 members in Germany). The Christian Press Academy offers month-long courses to young people interested in entering the field of journalism, and conducts frequent conferences where editors discuss religious, social, and cultural questions. The Radio and Television Academy arranges conferences for workers in communications media. The

Evangelical Action Committee for Labor Questions, organized in 1951, serves as a central research and information agency to serve churches and other groups throughout the country. It publishes a monthly magazine, *Mitarbeit,* which continues the information service formerly emanating from the Friedewald social academy. The conferences sponsored by these three agencies are held first at one place, then another; hence the "floating" designation.

There can be no doubt that the free and open atmosphere prevailing in academy discussions, and the firm reputation they have won as institutions concerned to serve the people, have won a new respect for the church from people long antagonistic or indifferent to its claims, or contemptuous of the role it has played in German life. In the process, the church has gained a new perspective on herself and her role in society. As one observer put it, "The church has rediscovered the world, and the world has rediscovered the church." Undoubtedly much of the credit for that rediscovery lies in the dialogue method employed—a startling departure in a society where the authoritative approach has long held sway. A Bad Boll pamphlet puts it this way: "Discussions have a warming and life-giving force if their purpose is not the intellectual liquidation of opponents, but communication between those jointly seeking answers. In a cooperative society, the cultivation of such discussion is increasingly demonstrating its vitality as the decisive instrument for the nurture of freedom and of man himself." And from Eberhard Müller: "The maintenance of freedom today, and indeed the continued existence of humanity, demands more than ever the ministry of the Church. To pioneer and develop this ministry is the fundamental aim of the Protestant Academies."[2]

---

[2] Weber, ed., *Signs of Renewal,* p. 11.

IV

THE NETHERLANDS: MUTUAL REDISCOVERY

For a century before World War II the Protestant churches of the Netherlands—Reformed, mainly, plus branches broken off the main trunk as the result of doctrinal disputes—had been drawing ever more closely in upon themselves. Their primary concerns were internal doctrinal and administrative matters, not what went on outside their doors, and the constant dwindling of attendance at their formal worship services disturbed them little.

Meanwhile, wrenching changes were taking place in the lives of the Dutch people. For one thing, their number was soaring: from three million as the twentieth century opened to nine million in 1940. To support the increase, the nation's leaders set out deliberately to foster industrialization. With that change in national direction, a traditionally agricultural, trading, and seafaring people was fast becoming subject to all the pressures of an industrial society—depersonalization, loss of individual initiative, and divorce from reassuring rural foundations. Some were being attracted by Marxist and other materialist ideologies. To many, the Christian faith of their fathers had come to have little attraction, little real meaning.

Then came World War II, and the stresses of daily life were intensified. But in their efforts to counteract the strictures of the occupying Nazis, the people developed new appreciation of values long neglected. The church was one organization which refused to be cowed by Nazi demands. Thus she began to win new respect not only from her merely nominal members, but from people who had never before paid her any mind. Since the Nazis forbade meetings of more than twenty persons, laymen began to come together in little groups, driven to seek answers to the problems posed by the presence of widespread evil. Many who had been indifferent became interested in the church's claims. On her own side the church began to show signs of being aware of, and concerned for, what went on outside her self-imposed boundaries. Thus the ground was prepared for seeds of renewal, planted at the end of the war by men peculiarly able to see and proclaim the need for such renewal.

Imprisoned in Buchenwald for his opposition to Nazi decrees, Johan Eykman, director of the Amsterdam Young Men's Christian Society, pondered this question: What had brought about the debasement of the German people, shown in the character of the men bringing degradation to his own country and in his brutalized captors? Like Hanns Lilje and other Germans asking themselves the same question in other prison cells about the same time, Dr. Eykman came to the conclusion that somehow the German church had failed to make her message implicit in the lives of her people. And he asked himself fearfully if the same sort of tragedy might not ensue among his own people if the churches continued to isolate themselves from the mainstream of Dutch life.

A similar fear had grown in the mind of another Dutch layman imprisoned in Germany as he sought to analyze the disaster of the mid-twentieth century. Hendrik Kraemer had refused the Nazis' request that he take a civilian post under their direction. Instead, he opposed their strictures openly and suffered the expected consequences. He had had a notable career as a lay missionary in Indonesia, as a professor of world religions in a Dutch university, and as a scholar in the language and literature of the East. Now, laying part of the blame for the outcropping of demonic forces in the civilized West on the gap between church and world, he resolved to find a way to help repair the breach. Released from Buchenwald at the end of the war, he led a group of Dutch churchmen in a determined effort to implement his resolution. Recalling the stand Dutch churches had made during the occupation, they hoped to insure that, though the people might fight for or against the church, they could never again be indifferent to her.

KERK EN WERELD

These Dutch churchmen—mostly laymen—approached church officials to argue that the nation's ecclesiastical life must be changed radically; that the day was past when the church could shut herself off from the people in street and factory, farm and dockyard. Some officials demurred, hesitant to jeopardize securities and privileges based on ecclesiastical tradition, which they felt must be preserved at all cost. But the views of the advocates of experimentation prevailed. They were granted funds from the state-collected church taxes which had accumulated during wartime, and could proceed with efforts to discover new types of approach to the laity. With part of the money they purchased "De Horst," a beech-shaded estate on the outskirts of Driebergen, a quiet town near Utrecht. There they established "Kerk en Wereld," a "church and world" institute, as the fountainhead of a movement dedicated (1) to fostering an apostolic spirit within the Dutch Reformed Church; (2) to linking church and world in mutual understanding, concern, and action; and (3) to training a lay leadership which would be the arm of the church in her efforts to become an effective force in the life of the nation.

The dream of the founders, most of them still active in the movement, has been realized to an extent greater than any of them dared anticipate fifteen years ago. Today Kerk en Wereld's influence extends into all areas of Dutch life. The original building, set back from the street beyond a curving drive, now houses a school of social work accredited by the government. At this Christian institution young men and women from all over the Netherlands, along with some from abroad, pursue a four-year course in preparation for service as Wikas, a new kind of church worker. After thorough studies in theology, psychology, sociology, and philosophy—as well as group and individual case work, plus practical training in art, crafts, folk dancing, music, and athletics—they go out to serve in parish and social centers, on church staffs in new or changing communities, in villages where industry is introducing a new way of life, in human relations programs in factories, in civic centers—wherever an opportunity is to be found. In the "big woods" behind De Horst, where families lease cottages and youth groups camp out in tent areas during the summer months, a future Wika gets practical experience by directing craft work, games, and athletic programs, and by leading discussion and worship groups.

In nearby Eykman House, whose construction was aided by gifts from American Presbyterians, conferences are held during the summer and in winter holiday periods under the direction of a permanent staff of experts. The building's spreading wings provide conference rooms and ample living and dining facilities. Some of the conferences, intended for already committed Christian laymen, offer Bible study, discussion of personal and social ethics, training in methods of evangelism, and consideration of the nature of the church. Others bring together theologians and members of various lay professions: teachers, physicians, nurses, economists, artists, journalists, and businessmen. In a special six-month course, personnel directors from business and industry come to Eykman House one week out of every four to study and discuss the spiritual foundations on which sound and creative human relationships can be built.

During the winter, except for holidays, the facilities are used by students from the Dutch theological faculties as they pursue intensive studies in church-and-world concerns.

In 1959, Kerk en Wereld established an extension institute program, one phase of which is the conducting of discussion and training sessions in industrial centers under the direction of a staff member. In each center, sessions are held for five successive week ends. They bring together people engaged in industry at all levels—personnel directors, executives, foremen, laborers, technicians—for serious discussion of human relationships on the job. Kerk en Wereld leaders are greatly encouraged by the enthusiastic response to another facet of the program: a "theory-plus-training" course for ministers who serve parishes in industrial communities, offered in cooperation with the theological faculty of the University of Utrecht. In still another part of the extension plan, a series of carefully planned "encounters" has been arranged between pastors and members of the strong Netherlands trade-union movement.

OUD POELGEEST

Today, eight other lay centers in the Netherlands conduct programs somewhat along the lines followed at Kerk en Wereld, but on a smaller scale. At Oegstgeest, a suburb of the university city of Leiden, the center known as Oud Poelgeest carries on an imaginative conference program in a charmingly restored thirteenth-century "castle" poised on the bank of an ancient canal, in a renovated coach house a few hundred yards away, and in a sleek new residence-and-meeting building set deep in an adjoining beech wood. Oud Poelgeest's director, A. W. Kist, is also a director of Kerk en Wereld and, increasingly, the programs and leadership of the two centers are being coordinated for more efficient and comprehensive dealing with current public issues.

At Oud Poelgeest, however, the emphasis is less on training leaders for parish and community service than on building bridges of acquaintance between church and culture, between people from different national and ecclesiastical backgrounds. At least half the sixty or so week-long courses offered annually are designed to give members of specific vocational groups a better understanding of their particular work in its relation to society, as well as an appreciation of the possibilities for self-realization and service through that work.

Oud Poelgeest is consciously ecumenical and international. During the year, five "International Weeks" bring together people in the same profession from various European countries to discuss common problems and to evaluate their own nations' international relations. Each summer an ecumenical youth conference attracts young people from a variety of church backgrounds and countries. Another particlularly creative "week" provides needed exchange between Dutch and German youth who, in discussing current political problems and mutual interests, discover that traditional antipathies disappear. The guest book in the castle lobby sparkles with comments—some in elaborate pictorial form—in which the young Germans have shown appreciation for their experiences of understanding, reconciliation, and just plain fun.

Besides the week-long conferences, Oud Poelgeest arranges many special week-end gatherings to explore specific themes of special interest. A random listing of titles from the schedule for one year indicates their scope: "Urban Expansion," "Aged People," "The Thought of Martin Buber," "The World Is Larger Than Europe," "What Is Left of Man's Self in Today's World?" "What Does Prosperity Do to Man?" "The World of Modern Poetry," "National State and European Order," "A Meeting with Three Modern Muses," and "A Meeting with Ouborg, a Modern Dutch Painter." From time to time, in cooperation with a group of economics experts, Oud Poelgeest brings industrial managers to its conference rooms to discuss what might be done to lessen the danger of depersonalization accompanying assembly line procedures.

Throughout, the Oud Poelgeest program makes room among its more sober preoccupations for creative activities—music, drama dance, sports, arts, and crafts—carried on in the evenings and during daytime breaks.

OTHER CENTERS

Though the smaller Dutch centers associated with the Federation of Lay Training Centers (mainly Reformed) have similar aims and methods, they differ in size, scope, and emphasis. For instance, Den Alerdinck, at Heino in the northeast part of the country, stresses rural problems. The district it serves includes the broad, sparsely settled *polder* (farmland reclaimed from the Zuider Zee). Hedenesse, in Zeeland, is particularly concerned with helping people prepare for rapid industrialization; for the rural, isolated peninsulas and islands lying in the Rhine delta will soon be united by the diking project now under way which will make the vast area the site of a great manufacturing complex.

Though the centers' leaders are careful to point out that their approach is not a sole or complete answer to the need for the churches to fulfill their mission in the world of today, they acknowledge that it "may have possibilities." There are signs that their estimate is too modest. One has only to visit a few of the new creative enterprises which are forging links between Dutch church and culture to encounter evidence that their inspiration and support have come from the lay centers.

That is so, for instance, in the weekday social centers established in some of the modern churches going up in new housing areas on the periphery of the larger cities. These centers—somewhat on the order of American settlement houses—represent a radical departure from the traditional in Dutch church life. Helping direct their programs are Wikas from Kerk en Wereld, where their training prepared them for just such service.

EXPERIMENTAL CHURCH ENTERPRISES

The influence is present, also, in some of these churches' experiments in bringing the congregation into vital participation in worship by introducing symbolic liturgical changes into the stark Dutch patterns. One church in a growing Amsterdam suburb has been so designed that attention is focused on a wooden cross towering over a communion table surrounded by benches on which the communicants sit. The pastor stands behind the table during the preliminary part of the worship service, and when it is time for the intercessory prayer he walks down from the chancel and kneels among the people. All this is far from traditional, and it symbolizes the lay-center-inspired concern for closer participation by the people in the total life of the churches. The people in the new housing areas, few of whom were active in the churches of their former parishes, welcome the innovations; they are coming to feel, their pastors have observed, that the church and its ministries are peculiarly their own. People who have rediscovered the church as a source of inspiration for their daily lives crowd the services.

For the past six years, the Dutch Reformed, *Gereformeerde,* Lutheran, Old Catholic, and Remonstrant churches—as well as the Salvation Army—have joined in conducting a pilot industrial chaplaincy in a number of the Netherlands' urban areas. "Of course, all along we got ideas and encouragement from the staff at Kerk en Wereld," the young men staffing that chaplaincy point out as they recall the difficult early days when the idea for such a venture had not yet been fully accepted. These young pastors had come to realize that, in its traditional form, the Dutch parish church was not meeting the peculiar needs of the industrial worker, mired in the humdrum, aimless, and deadening round of daily life, for guiding principles in coping with a milieu where competition—the key word—causes frustration and disregard for the fellow worker. The industrial worker was walking past the closed door of the parish church — the "pastor's church"— and neither he nor the church seemed to care. With help from Kerk en Wereld and other lay centers, the pilot chaplaincy got under way; today it is a firmly established project, ecumenically governed and financed.

Under the new program, the industrial pastors live among the working people, mingle with them on their time off, visit them in their homes, talk about immediate concerns. Eventually the discussion gets around to religious principles. When enough men show interest in continuing discussion, the pastors arrange for groups of a dozen or so workers—managers and technicians, too, if possible—to meet in someone's home. At the start, newcomers are skeptical. What does religion have to do with a man's job? But before long they find themselves deep in discussion about what it would mean if a man were really to live as a Christian. Eventually, someone asks if he can't try starting another group; he knows several men who would welcome the chance to get things off their chests in honest man-to-man debate.

Thus the growth-out-of-growth proceeds—"like strawberry plants," as one industrial chaplain puts it, recalling that before the great factories were built in his own area it was all one vast strawberry plantation. The chaplaincy is constantly seeking men particularly fitted by personality, interest, and dedication for work of this nature. As soon as possible, they are given the opportunity to take special training in the nature and problems of modern industry, then assigned to new program centers. The general agency through which the six denominations share in support and supervision of the program reports that about forty per cent of the men it reaches have never before had any contacts with church life of any kind. The lay centers continue to aid the project, training the men who carry out the ideas, providing resources which determine what the greatest problems are and what procedures are most likely to result in workable solutions. At the lay centers' industrial conferences, the newly interested are able to see the wider implications of their problems and gain perspective on the relation of the Christian faith to their own perplexities.

In still other areas of Dutch life there are tentative signs of a new development of mutual appreciation between the church and secular institutions. Much of Netherlands society has long been set in confessional molds: Protestant and Catholic schools, Protestant and Catholic political parties, Protestant and Catholic newspapers. But in recent years the designations have served mainly as labels. Today the liveliest and most perceptive reporting of religious news—critical sometimes, but as often appreciative—is found not in the traditionally denominational papers but in the Socialist party's daily newspaper. Before the war, the Socialist party was to a great extent anti-Christian. Since its end a new rapport has grown up, and in the party's ranks—even in its leadership—are to be found many churchmen, both Protestant and Catholic. Increasingly, laymen are discovering that it is in the world, not in isolated groups labeled "Christian" alone, that their Christian witness is to be made.

In the cultural world of the Netherlands a movement has made headway, during the past decade, in fostering creative encounter between the church and the arts: architecture, sculpture, poetry, drama, painting, and music. Its fruits are to be seen in the contemporary design and decoration—among the most striking in Europe today—of the new churches of the suburbs and reclaimed land, as well as in the increasing interest of Dutch artists in religious themes. A Tuesday evening service held in an Amsterdam church weekly attracts some three hundred people from the art world who have had no previous connection whatever with religion; they take part in an experiment to translate the various arts into elements of worship. There are study circles where pastors and lay officials engaged in building projects meet with architects and decorative artists to exchange ideas, argue, try to interpret to each other their standards, aims, guiding principles—and limitations.

No Dutch churchman claims that a revolutionary break has been made through the curtain of unconcern that, for a century, has threatened to make of the Netherlands churches a realm apart. But the energetic measures taken by men who sensed what devastation such separation might induce have begun a penetration that in the days ahead may well widen into a decisive breach.

V

THE EUROPEAN SCENE: PATHS TO ENCOUNTER

FRANCE

Of the forty-three million inhabitants of France, only about one million are Protestants (most Reformed, some Lutheran). They are scattered among a majority which, while nominally Roman Catholic, is so imbued with the spirit of secularism—in many cases so anticlerical—that the Roman hierarchy has been known to acknowledge that for all practical purposes France is a mission field.

Perhaps because of the inner tensions within French Catholicism, perhaps because of the liberal spirit cherished by all Frenchmen, Protestants in France today—unlike their ancestors—do not suffer the harassments or civil disabilities besetting minority faiths in certain other nominally Catholic countries. But they have their problems. Though they provide a disproportionate number of leaders in the intellectual world, many of the rank and file live in isolated rural communities and have little chance to associate with other Protestants. And they are subject to all the modern-day stresses that exist throughout the civilized West. To overcome that aloneness and that pressure, the French Reformed Church has in recent years embarked on a number of ventures with aims and methods parallel in certain respects to those of other European lay centers. Here there is no need to reforge ties between churches and nominal members grown indifferent and estranged, as in Germany, say, or Sweden; and the French Protestant churches cherish no illusions about exerting a decisive influence on a society in which they are so definitely a minority. But they do live and work in the world of the majority and there, as laymen, they meet situations calling for interpretation and insight.

In a number of the larger French cities, Protestants have set up associations along vocational or professional lines. Within them, lay men and women consider their role in making the church manifest in the workaday world. In Paris, a Christian training center was established in 1952 as a place where members of a scattered minority could become more responsible bearers of witness. CIMADE, the imaginative and effective French Protestant youth program which came into being during World War II as an agency for extending aid to Jews and other victims of Nazi persecution—both Frenchmen and foreign refugees—continues to offer young people an opportunity to render sacrificial service.

At Glay, in an industrial area near the Swiss and German borders, French Reformed churchmen opened a lay training center in 1952. There people from widely separated parishes may discover that their churches are not isolated cells. They profit from exchange of ideas and mutual encouragement, discuss with fellow workers the problems and pressures of their jobs, consider together all manner of public issues, and take part in practical experiments looking toward new forms of church life.

Glay also makes it possible for laymen to have profitable encounters with people outside the French Reformed Church. Reports tell of repeated conferences between French and German churchmen, arranged in cooperation with the Bad Boll Evangelical Academy, at which brotherhood and understanding are given a chance to replace the bitterness left by World War II. Other conferences bring to Glay people from the secular mainstream of French life to confer with churchmen, Reformed and Lutheran, on public issues. At one such conference over one hundred women discussed the controversial subject of birth control. A non-Christian attorney who as a member of the French parliament had introduced a birth-control bill, learned for the first time (from an address by a Reformed pastor) that some Christian concepts of the role of sex in family life may differ from those expounded by Roman Catholics.

Many families in the area are given the opportunity to spend their holidays in a Christian atmosphere at Glay. A similar opportunity exists at a camp center at Le Nouvion, in northern France, where evangelism has a part in the program. Here, too, "cross-road meetings" are held on eight week ends of the year for people in the widely scattered Protestant parishes in the area. The reports of those meetings are assembled and later distributed to the parishes.

In June, 1960, the Church of the Augsburg Confession of Alsace and Lorraine (Lutheran) officially inaugurated a lay center, Liebfrauenberg, in Strasbourg. Already thirteen conferences had been held since March, when the program got under way with an "ecumenical colloquium" between Lutheran and Reformed theologians.

A French institution which combines the functions of spiritual retreat and conference center came into being in 1954 in the Community of Villemétrie, centering on a manor house in the countryside not far from Paris. In permanent residence there are a number of men who lead an ordered life of work, study, and worship. Coming to the center for frequent discussions of the significance and the problems of their vocations are people from key positions in the nation's life: civic employees, artists, theatrical workers, scientists, and economists. Considerable theological study and research are carried on as well. Not infrequently, Roman Catholics participate in the discussions—a situation less to be marveled at in France than in other predominantly Catholic lands.

Two news reports chosen at random from those issuing from the center in the spring of 1959 reveal the variety of "church and world" encounters Villemétrie makes possible. Periodically, a number of French physicists have been meeting at the manor house to discuss the ethical questions to which their work gives rise. After one spring meeting they joined in appealing to the Federation of French Protestant Churches to set up a commission of theologians, politicians, and scientists which would undertake systematic study of the relation of the Christian faith to problems raised by nuclear weapons. They proposed three questions with which such a commission might begin: (1) Is there a point at which scientific research oversteps the limits imposed by God on man at the time of creation? (2) Can technological progress be continued indefinitely without becoming a menace to the humanity of man? (3) May not atomic warfare prove to be a form of anarchy rather than a means of maintaining order? Then the physicists, speaking out of what was obviously deep spiritual unease, put their dilemma to the churches. They felt that the churches are obliged to help the scientists among their membership, especially those with conscience pangs about their work, to discover their Christian responsibility in this situation. And, speaking more boldly, "In our opinion, the church of Christ should proclaim the message of peace entrusted to it, and refuse to submit to any illusory political consideration."

In April, the Villemétrie center was host to a conference representing a unique concern, the spiritual welfare of men and women of many nationalities who work in one or another of the sprawling complex of international organizations with headquarters in Paris: UNESCO, NATO, UNICEF, WEU, and others. One Anglican layman there, keenly aware of the difficulty of being a Christian when away from accustomed roots and surrounded by vocally cynical and irreligious co-workers, had attempted, a year earlier, to find some way for laymen with the same feeling to come together on a "horizontal" basis—across denominational lines. Working with pastors of the few Protestant churches in Paris, seeking counsel from the World Council of Churches, Department on the Laity, he kept at it until a little circle of Protestants, along with some Roman Catholics, was meeting regularly for worship and discussion. At Villemétrie they held their first retreat, sharing in worship and meditation, gaining theological insights from presentations by church leaders who were able to illuminate the puzzling aspects of their dilemma, finding further clarification in subsequent discussions. Thus Villemétrie served as a source of strength for people set down in a milieu where they are a minority, even as is Protestantism itself in France.

At Taizé, in Burgundy, is one of the small number of Protestant retreat centers established in recent years, centers which reflect other lay enterprises' concern for church renewal, if not for church-world encounter. The permanent community at Taizé, established twenty years ago, is made up of about forty Lutheran and Reformed "brothers"—some ordained clergymen, others laymen. Sharing a rule of poverty, chastity, and obedience, they live in an old manor house, with a chapel nearby and accommodations for guests who come for retreat periods of varying length. They work on the farm and in the shops on the property, follow a regular schedule of worship, and carry on study and research, with emphasis on church unity. Roman Catholics of irenic bent are frequent guests. Interesting liturgical experiments in recovery of ancient choral music and employment of contemporary forms appear in the daily worship periods. The laymen in the group live under vows but follow their own trades or professions; some are craftsmen, some farmers—one is a physician who practices in the surrounding rural area. In a missionary extension of the work, teams of brothers live where people endure hardships—in the slums of Algiers, Marseilles, or Paris—seeking to effect reconciliation by prayer and service. Teams go out, too, to spend time serving on the staffs of Protestant lay centers; in the fall of 1959, two of the men began a period of residence at Packard Manse (see p. 117), a lay venture near Boston. In the summer of 1960, the Taizé community launched a conference center in the nearby village of Cormatin, where people from varied backgrounds consider the reasons for Christian divisions and discuss Christian responsibility in social and economic problems, political issues, and racial tensions.

ITALY

Retreats also play an important part in the program of Agape, the ecumenical village in the heart of northern Italy's mountainous country, long the stronghold of that nation's hardy Waldensians. Built by young people from all confessions and from all parts of the world joining in a series of work camps, Agape is host during the summer to a wide variety of meetings which demonstrate the center's concern for the practice of Christian love, service, and brotherhood. But during the winter, except for week ends, the facilities are open to anyone—Christian or non-Christian—who feels the need for meditation, relaxation, study, or spiritual renewal. The staff provides counsel only when counsel is requested.

FINLAND

As there are indications that the state Lutheran Church of Finland is now moving slowly from a clerical to a people's church, two training institutes for laymen have come into being there—Järvenpää, for the ninety per cent of the population which is Finnish-speaking, and Lärkulla, at Kaaris, for those who speak Swedish. Since opportunity for voluntary service has increased in the parishes, the centers offer training in religion, health, and social welfare to prepare men and women for that service. As at Sigtuna, in Sweden, the centers are associated with "people's colleges," where adult education, including religion courses, is available. All phases of the centers' activities are supported, spiritually and financially, by the Church of Finland.

In addition to their educational programs, which attract people who are already associated with parish churches, the centers sponsor a limited number of conferences intended to renew contacts with adults estranged from church life. Since, so far, no definite pattern of procedure has been worked out, the leaders are still feeling their way. At Järvenpää, two conferences were arranged for theologians and psychiatrists. Others have been held for teachers in agricultural colleges, for savings bank employees, and for directors of adult education enterprises. Finnish churchmen point out that, though ninety per cent of its population is Lutheran, Finland is in a unique relation to churches of the West and of the East; its Christian life began when missionaries from the West (Lutheran) and from the East (Orthodox) arrived to evangelize the region. So in recent years Järvenpää has been host to a number of meetings between representatives of the two traditions; the aim is to interpret each to the other and to consider jointly the churches' responsibility to society. At some of these conferences Protestant and Orthodox theologians from other European countries have been present. The buildings at the two centers symbolize the ties between Finnish Lutherans and Lutherans in the distant West. They were erected with the aid of funds contributed by the Finns' fellow churchmen in North America.

SWITZERLAND

Under an extremely autonomous ecclesiastical system, Protestant (Reformed) church life in Switzerland centers almost exclusively in the local congregation or, at most, in the local canton. Joint endeavors by groups of churches are, therefore, the exception rather than the rule. In recent years, however, meeting centers have been established in several of the autonomous synods (usually determined by the cantons' boundaries). Most of these *Heimstätte* (homes) are designed for church assemblies and youth meetings. In some cases they are operated by foundations independent of the ecclesiastical systems. One in particular lays special stress on laymen's enterprises—Boldern, near Männedorf, in the canton of Zurich.

Adequately housed and situated in pleasant rural surroundings, Boldern was founded in 1947 by a group of laymen and theologians led by Professor Emil Brunner of the University of Zurich's theological faculty. At first it was an independent venture, but after the experiment had proved its staying power the Zurich synod and individual parishes of the canton joined in supporting it. In addition to serving as a center for the congregations and lending its staff to direct local conferences, Boldern carries on a lively conference program for members of specific occupational groups and other interested laymen. In so doing, it proceeds much as do the German academies. Each conference is arranged by a preparatory team of laymen, members of the particular occupational group concerned. They draw up lists of potential participants; they decide in preliminary consultations what subjects will spark the most creative discussion. Among the many vocational groups which have met for conferences at Boldern are farmers, industrial workers, office clerks, retail store employees, contractors, architects, lawyers, doctors, and engineers.

As in other countries, organized labor in Switzerland has, on the whole, lost touch with the church. Recognizing this fact, Boldern arranges regular courses for trade-union members. It has been gratified in these sessions by the enthusiastic participation in Bible study and discussion of fundamental religious principles. At times, too, opportunity is provided for mutual discussion by workers and employers.

Throughout the whole program the staff at Boldern has discovered encouraging evidence that modern men and women, both within and outside the church, are welcoming the Christian gospel when it is presented in terms of man's own experience, and in language that has real meaning for the present day. Further, it has found among the newly interested a striking ability to translate that gospel—perhaps in startlingly untraditional manner—into terms applicable to their daily lives and vocational relationships.

INTERNATIONAL ORGANIZATIONS

Within and adjacent to Switzerland are certain church-and-world centers that have no relationship to the nation as such but which, like so many other institutions in that "neutral" land, serve the world at large. In the Castle Mainau, on an island in Lake Constance between Switzerland and Germany, the world and European alliances of Y.M.C.A.'s sponsor a continuing training program for Christian youth leaders. In recent years Mainau has added a function similar to that of the church-world institutes—it sponsors consultations wherein experts in various secular fields consider what it means to be Christian in the contemporary world. At Mainau, however, the question is approached from the viewpoint of youth pondering the impact on itself of the social, economic, and technological changes taking place in modern society. The themes of four consultations held during a recent summer indicate their direction: "Automation and Man," "What Is Meant by 'Materialistic Youth' in East and West?" "Youth, Politics, and the Christian Faith," and "The Witness of a Lay Movement." In addition, conferences were held that year on a variety of special themes ranging from "Family and Sex Questions" to "International Relations." Participants in the Mainau courses and conferences come mainly from Europe, but some young people are usually on hand from other continents; one year, twenty-four countries and three faiths—Protestant, Roman Catholic, and Orthodox—were represented.

In a quiet center at Clarens, Switzerland, the American Friends Service Committee each summer sponsors a series of international conferences little publicized but pregnant with possibilities for future good in world affairs. The ten-day affairs are attended by responsible government officials who respond to the Quakers' invitation to talk over international affairs off the record and from a philosophical viewpoint. Usually, two sessions are conducted annually for diplomats, and since 1957 three meetings for parliamentarians have been held. So far, people from fifty-two countries—including, by the way, Czechoslovakia, Yugoslavia, Poland, Rumania, Hungary, and the U.S.S.R.—have gathered at Clarens. With no decisions dependent on what is said, the conferences have produced realistic exchange of viewpoints and some understanding—above all, the realization that behind the increasingly mechanical moves and countermoves of diplomatic and parliamentary procedures lie human relationships. The Quakers hope that from the seeds planted at Clarens may grow wisdom, comprehension, and forbearance to temper national and international debate in the years to come.

Spacious, tree-shaded Château de Bossey, just outside the village of Céligny on the western side of mountain-rimmed Lake Geneva, houses a clergy and lay training center whose functions are those of all the others writ large. The Ecumenical Institute at Bossey is closely related to the World Council of Churches, whose headquarters are just a half-hour's ride away at Geneva.

Two years before the World Council formally came into being (at Amsterdam, in 1948), the institute was set up to aid in the renewal of the church throughout the world by helping to prepare the laity (ninety-nine per cent of her membership) to be effective witnesses to her message and to bridge the gap between church and world. In addition, it was commissioned to conduct research on issues concerning church unity.

From the day its doors opened, the facilities of the Ecumenical Institute at Bossey have been heavily used. Until 1954, the program was directed by Hendrik Kraemer, who had so much to do with the founding of Kerk en Wereld in the Netherlands. His contention was that the laity constitutes the church's "frozen assets," and the program he inspired was intended to free those assets. When he retired, the directorship was taken over by H. H. Wolf.

A gift from John D. Rockefeller, Jr., enabled the World Council to lease the château for five years. Then, aided by subsequent gifts

s in a religious drama nted at the Sigtuna dation in Sweden

ents at Bad Boll acad- in Germany look on as tor is interviewed for broadcast

Unique chapel of the Evangelical Acad of Hessen/Nassau, at Arnoldshain in Taunus mountains of Germany

Austere, modern interior of the chape the Kerk en Wereld institute "de Hc in Driebergen, the Netherlands

George MacLeod (far left, below) leads procession on the Isle of Iona, Great Britain

from the same source, it was able to purchase the entire sixty-eight-acre estate, modernize the eighteenth century mansion, and erect houses for the staff. Adjoining an ancient round tower at the end of the wing of the château nearest the lake, an unusual chapel has been constructed; near the top of the tower stands a smaller auxiliary chapel. In the château are spacious conference rooms and offices, an extensive library, and living and dining facilities for about eighty guests. Since participants come to Bossey from all parts of the world, conference rooms are equipped for simultaneous translations of talks—in English, French, and German.

In its leaders' words, the Ecumenical Institute seeks to be "a place of pioneer thinking and ecumenical encounter." They explain, "Bossey deliberately seeks to bring about the meeting between people of different races, color, language, and Christian confession; but this ecumenical encounter is not merely [that] carried on at the level of the large World Council of Churches' assemblies such as Amsterdam, in 1948, or Evanston, in 1954, where often it is limited to theologians and other ecclesiastical dignitaries, but within smaller and more intimate courses and conferences where the most ordinary church members can play a part. Indeed, it is the prime purpose of Bossey to help these church members realize that they *are* the Church. Because of this, Bossey tries to show church members their responsibility to the World: 'God was in Christ reconciling *the world* to Himself.' To be in the Church means to bear responsibility for a reconciling ministry within the world, and this should mean a readiness to face the problems which are posed to the Church by the social and political cultures in which it is set. Bossey tries to present those who come to its courses with the challenge offered to the Church by a secular world which is, nevertheless, God's world. Finally, Bossey seeks to bring this about within the context of worship and with common Bible study at the center of every course or conference, for it works in the conviction that only as we are prepared to place ourselves again under the judgment of God's Word can the Church truly be renewed; and it is as Christians see their need for renewal that they begin to catch a glimpse of a unity that transcends all present divisions and which is Christ's call to His Church."[1]

Each summer Bossey offers special two- and three-week courses for ministers, missionaries, theological students, and laymen from all over the world and all confessions. Together they worship, study the Bible, and consider the problems confronting the church. In addition, Bossey sponsors, throughout the year, a program of short vocational conferences at which doctors, nurses, lawyers, artists, businessmen, journalists—people from various walks of life, but particularly the professions—talk over the dilemmas posed by conflicts between their work and their Christian faith. Thus the conferences reproduce, on an international scale, the "man and his job" discussions which are so typical a feature of the European lay academies. More complex, concentrated, and academic are the research and thinking that go on in a third facet of the Bossey program—the consultations and study conferences at which experts confer on questions which demand informed, pioneer exploration. Subject matter must be pertinent to man's need and to the present hour. Recent consultation themes have ranged from the roots of juvenile delinquency to the philosophical basis of reality and on to the social implications of nuclear power.

Still another phase of the work at Bossey is the Graduate School of Ecumenical Studies, which was established in 1952 in cooperation with the University of Geneva's theological faculty. Two semester courses are offered each year. In them, students who have completed university courses in theology or other academic disciplines probe more deeply into aspects of church unity and the contemporary witness of the church than is possible in the shorter summer courses and conferences. Lectures are given by institute staff members, visiting professors from universities and theological

---

[1] *The Ecumenical Institute* (Folder issued by the World Council of Churches, Geneva).

seminaries in various countries, and staff members of the World Council of Churches.

From its inception Bossey has had close ties with the lay centers throughout Europe. Many of them have drawn inspiration from its conferences and its findings, and vice versa. Their leaders are often at Bossey for conferences, individually and in groups. Yet the centers and the institute developed independently, both reflections of a widespread concern for realistic and creative involvement by the churches in the problems of the modern world.

Since 1955, the European lay centers have been loosely united in a Directors' Association of the Laymen's Colleges in Europe, with headquarters at Bad Boll in Germany. In annual meetings and in correspondence the association facilitates helpful exchange of experiences and information, strengthens the work of individual centers, and encourages the development of a philosophy that will enable them all to undergo whatever stresses and difficulties may arise in the future.

EUROPEAN LAY ASSEMBLIES

Dramatizing, for the public at large, the impetus lay witness has made among European Protestants in recent years, the churches of Germany, France, the Netherlands, and Scotland have developed a new type of lay assembly. The German word Kirchentag is used as a generic term for this type of assembly. Kirchentag was the name given to the nineteenth-century church congresses assembled to hear the call for renewal by J. H. Wichern that resulted in the Inner Mission movement. It has been revived, a century later, to designate not only the German assembly, but also the French Rassemblement Protestant, the Dutch Kerk Dagen, and the Scottish Kirk Week. In each case, Protestants from a specific region or an entire nation gather for a series of lectures, Bible study, small-group discussion, and a program of song and drama—all centering on some aspect of modern man's involvement with the world about him.

The German Kirchentag, pioneer of the modern assemblies and by far the most ambitious and comprehensive, brings together hundreds of thousands of Protestants from all over Germany, plus a growing contingent from abroad. In a way, it ties together in one week the strands of all the efforts being made throughout the nation for renewal of the church: theological and social studies, philanthropic services, student chaplaincies, drama and music, and the academy program of church-world encounter. It is particularly effective in broadening the viewpoint of members of the regional German churches, long accustomed to think of their church in terms of their particular areas only. Not only national but world-wide concerns of Christianity and of man are dealt with in the Kirchentag.

Beginning in a small way in Hannover, soon after World War II, the movement quickly caught on. The Kirchentag was held annually from 1950 to 1954, then scheduled biannually. The 1958 meeting planned for the Soviet zone had to be postponed after government authorities withdrew approval, and the next was held at Munich, in the western zone, in 1959. In 1950, twenty-five thousand Protestants from all over Germany attended daily sessions of the first national Kirchentag, at Essen, and two hundred thousand participated in the great outdoor worship service with which the week ended. At Leipzig, in the eastern zone, sixty thousand people gathered for the daily sessions in 1954, six hundred thousand for the closing service; approximately the same number participated in the assembly at Frankfort on the Main, again in the West, in 1956. At the Munich Kirchentag, in 1959, special arrangements were made for participation by "ecumenical visitors" from abroad, with small English-language sessions at which those unfamiliar with the German language were helped to grasp the significance of what was going on.

The Kirchentag's roots lie in the Wichern awakening and in the "Protestant Weeks" of the 1930's. Those "weeks" were part of the program by which the "confessing church" sought to crystallize sentiment against Nazi-imposed restrictions. Members of the "councils of brethren"— cells made up of protesting pastors, theologians, and laymen—came together in order to join in worship and find inspiration in fellowship that would help them carry on their lonely and sometimes dangerous resistance to Nazi tyranny.

The present embodiment of the Kirchentag owes its inception and much of its momentum to Reinold von Thadden-Trieglaff, a sturdy layman who had been much influenced in his university days by the Student Christian Movement. Member of a prominent land-holding family in Pomerania, he became a leader in the anti-Hitler resistance of the churches in that eastern region. In 1945, the Russians sent him to Siberia as a civilian internee. His experiences there, his fellowship with men representing all kinds of attitudes, convinced him that only by humble and honest searching with Christians and non-Christians, with pious men and rationalists, could churchmen discover an effective way to make the Christian gospel come alive in society. After returning to Germany at the end of the war, he found an outlet for his convictions when he was asked to undertake a mission for the World Council of Churches—visiting German prisoners of war in Allied camps. Later, as a participant in the work of the Ecumenical Institute at Bossey, he learned about the lay programs in the churches of Great Britain and North America. At once he set about to discover a vehicle for active lay work which would attract the attention of Protestants throughout Germany. The result was the Kirchentag movement, which has occupied his waking moments ever since. Writing recently in a World Council of Churches booklet describing the movement, von Thadden analyzed its purposes thus:

"[It] has set itself the task to call Protestant lay Christians to their responsibilities in all sectors of public life and to make them active, particularly in the economic, social, and political fields where Christian principles are on trial and where Christian obedience has to stand the test. The layman is anything but some sort of marginal figure on the outskirts of the Church. He is *the essential interpreter of the Christian message in the battlefield of the world.* Therefore he must be spiritually prepared for open confession of his faith, and for active service in *everyday life as well as in the Church congregation.* . . . The Kirchentag . . . is not a meeting of elected representatives of the Church: it aims at bringing together the voluntary lay forces in Germany. It has no membership—and no records from which to register what it has achieved. The Kirchentag is not, and does not want to be, a church itself. Its nature cannot be understood in isolation from the Church, but only in relation to it. It is, and wishes to remain, a spontaneous and voluntary contribution to the building up of the Church. It has no party program on national or international problems, or on political or ideological differences. But within the limits of our specifically Christian obedience, it seeks to make clear to all people the responsibility of the Church in the spheres of present world and national issues."[2]

In its final mass meeting, preceded by parades and featured by inspirational addresses and a great outpouring of song, the Kirchentag makes its greatest impact on the general public, locally and in the nation at large. At first this "mass" element led to some eyebrow-raising; had not Germany had more than her share of mass-manipulation at the hands of the Nazis? True, acknowledged the Kirchentag leaders, but that need not discredit the method itself; the churches' purpose was not to manipulate or exploit, but to provide convinced Christians, often dispirited by apparent isolation in an indifferent culture, an experience of spiritual fellowship and inspiration along with others in like situations.

Despite the play given the final rally in press and popular reports, the most lasting results of the Kirchentag emanate, rather, from the weeklong discussion and Bible study, and from the months of preparatory study that have preceded the gathering. Groups of

---

[2] Reinold von Thadden-Trieglaff, "The Origins of the German Kirchentag," in *Meet the Church* (Geneva: World Council of Churches, Department on the Laity, 1959), p. 6.

men and women have considered the themes for the Kirchentag's discussion sessions in the light of their own experience and current national and international issues. Then, during the week of meetings, they gather daily in working groups of manageable size for frank and critical probing of pertinent questions. Here, for instance, are some of the themes discussed at Munich in 1959: "How Can Modern Man Live with the Church?" "How Can a Christian Family Life Be Lived Today?" "What Has God to Do with Modern Industry?" "What About the Church in Relation to the Mass Media: Television, Film, Radio?" "Of What Does 'Mission Work' Consist in Today's World?" The aim of the discussion sessions is not to produce conformity in ideas and attitudes, but to encourage creative thought, honest appraisal of problems, and a Christian approach to personal and political relationships. Still another aspect of the Kirchentag shows a relationship between the church and art. There are striking exhibits of painting and sculpture, great concerts by choral and instrumental groups and by individual musicians, showings of films, and presentations of dramas.

A number of German cities carry out similar programs on a much smaller scale from time to time. Some of these "junior Kirchentags" follow a four-week schedule: one week devoted to preparation for later "visitations" (here an echo of North American "visitation evangelism"); the second week given to actual visitation in people's homes; the third featuring evening lectures, films, and discussion of current issues; the fourth including meetings within vocational groups, climaxed by a public rally. In other cities the program is condensed into a single week, sometimes into a few days. In all these efforts, however, the pattern of Bible study, discussion, and final rally is constant.

Impressed by the German example, the churches of the Netherlands have sponsored regional Church Days which embody similar ideas and methods on a much less ambitious scale. At first they were spontaneous, unrelated affairs. But since 1955, when leaders met at Kerk en Wereld to correlate their efforts, a permanent

Church Day Work Group has agreed on a common theme for regional observances and has published booklets with suggestions for preliminary study on those themes. By 1958, eight hundred of the some two thousand Dutch Reformed parishes were participating in the program, which aims to build up lay fellowship in the parishes, deepen faith in relation to life today, and inspire the laity to forge new contacts between God's Word and the world. The Church Days follow a common pattern: families in a given area come together to listen, worship, sing, and take part in religious dramas; then, in smaller groups, they discuss the given theme in the light of familiar situations. A fundamental concern of leaders in the movement is to foster the development of a "listening" church. They explain: "We must enter into and maintain a *conversation* with the world. We can only do this if we are . . . alert to hear what both God and God's world have to say to us. Christians who cannot listen stand in the way of their own witness; they [are unable to] obey God's command to be, as it were, a *mediator* between Him and His World."

In Scotland, seven Protestant denominations which had been working together in the continuing and many-pronged evangelism program "Tell Scotland" joined in 1957 to sponsor a Kirk Week in Aberdeen, "most authentic of Scottish cities." The program, consciously drawing on the German Kirchtentag pattern, was designed not as an evangelistic rally, but as a means of helping laymen discover how to make their faith operative in their daily lives. Each day of the week began with worship, followed by Bible study. Then came division into smaller study groups—seventy in all—led by specially trained laymen. The groups explored the critical contemporary issues set forth in formal addresses given the preceding evening to the entire assembly. Meanwhile, an exhibit of paintings and sculpture on religious themes was on view in the city's art galleries, talks were being given on current literature and films, concerts were presented in local music halls, and experimental social dramas were offered for entertainment and serious discussion.

In 1959, the second Scottish Kirk Week was held, in Dundee. The theme, "The Crisis of Man," concerned man in his total environment, in industry, in the family, in his taste and judgment; it was presented in formal addresses, again followed by small discussion groups. The goal was to translate the Word of God into action which would help lessen the impact of the current crises. As at Aberdeen, there were exhibits of painting, sculpture, and photographs, as well as concerts and dramatic presentations.

Leaders of Kirk Week point out that laymen, living and working in the midst of the stresses of modern society, are better fitted than the clergy to understand what is going on in that society. When brought together to scrutinize those problems critically, lay people open the way for interpretation of the Bible in modern terms. At the Aberdeen Kirk Week, in an effort to measure the usefulness of the layman in the church's mission, vocational work groups were established for people caught up in the problems of rural life, education, and industry. Out of their deliberations came relevant definitions of many of the pressures and tensions in these areas. After the week was over, leaders of the movement pointed out, "Perhaps the most significant development [was] an increasing awareness that ministry and laity are *one*—both are 'laos'—the people of God—with different kinds of ministry, but still one. Each needs the other, and no advance can be made unless there is the utmost cooperation and understanding between them."[3]

France, too, has had lay rallies inspired by the example of the Kirchentag. The first Rassemblement Protestant, in which Lutheran and Reformed churches join, was held in Strasbourg, near the German border, in 1956. It was preceded by study in local parishes of four preparatory booklets on the chosen theme, "The Lord Said, 'Where Is Thy Brother?' " Bible study was followed by group discussion of how the general theme could be applied, and by a final rally in which twenty thousand people heard calls to assume

[3] Colin Day, "Kirk Week in Scotland," in *Meet the Church,* p. 28.

personal responsibility for the achievement of reconciliation and brotherhood. The next year a similar Rassemblement Protestant was held in the west of France, at Royan. In preparation for that regional assembly, one hundred fifty local groups spent several months studying documents relating to six aspects of daily life in which "Living in Peace"—the theme for the Rassemblement—is threatened. Most of the discussion centered on problems raised by life in the small towns where most of the Protestants of western France live. From the preparatory work came perhaps the most creative result of the whole enterprise: for the first time, many lay men and women had acted on their own initiative, voiced their deepest concerns, without depending on their pastors to lead the way. In so doing, they had gained new realization of how their faith could be concretely applied to everyday experience. Such was not always the case, however; in some communities the preparation was done by little groups accustomed to carrying the parish program, with the pastor in total charge of what went on and what was said. But the degree of success in developing creative study by laymen was encouraging to leaders of the Rassemblement. The final rally, at Royan, was the extension and culmination of a winter of study, personal contact, prayer, and "new directions." Many non-Protestants attended the sessions, laymen spoke out on their own initiative, and reports growing out of joint study were subjected to question and comment by the whole assembly.

All in all, the German Kirchentag and its little brothers in France, Scotland, and the Netherlands constitute a dramatic demonstration of the vital concern which underlies the more deliberate and continuing programs of the lay centers. Another relationship between the centers and the Kirchentag is suggested by Mark Gibbs, British layman who served as chairman of the ecumenical committee for the 1959 German Kirchentag: "There is still a certain tendency . . . to encourage laymen to be some kind of imitation (and clearly inferior) ministers, instead of calling them to do their job as Christ's representatives in the world outside the Church. . . . We must develop a clearer understanding of our *theology* of the laity. Do we in any sense really accept the biblical doctrine of the *laos*—the whole people of God, with differences of function, so that people can specialize in being pastors, or teachers, or administrators, or housewives, or engineers, or artists, but with no monopoly of gifts to anyone? Or do we still give priority of status to the bishop or the business tycoon or the church or state official? It seems to me the superb justification of the Kirchentag movement that such questions were in Dr. von Thadden's mind from the very first. . . . I can only voice my personal concern, echoed I believe by many friends of both the Kirchentag and the academy movements in Europe, that the clergy may, with *the very best intentions,* kill the lay activities which they are earnestly trying to encourage, and [I] urge that they strive to leave the leadership—and sometimes the last words—to lay people. Of course, both in Britain and in Europe (perhaps less so in the United States) lay people are only too willing to leave everything to the parson, so that he must be the more concerned to educate us in our responsibilities. . . . I feel that it is a difficult and perhaps a dangerous venture to launch even a small Kirchentag without a cadre of keen, well-informed, and well-trained lay people. And here . . . is the great importance of the lay academies in Germany and in Europe. Such lay leaders are the more necessary because . . . a Kirchentag is *not* primarily a mass rally, but the culmination of a process of lay education, extending over several months. . . . It would make rather a dull and 'churchy' Kirchentag if *everybody* came as a delegate from local study groups. But the heart of the Kirchentag technique is preparation . . . and this . . . will be a complete failure if it becomes just another cozy parish group listening to the local priest or pastor. It is here that local laymen must be found, not only for recruiting and administration (again, so often left to the clergy) but also for chewing over in small groups the relevant Kirchentag themes and

Bible study passages."[4] In other words, laymen prepared and inspired by past association with such ventures as the academies in Germany, Kerk en Wereld and its fellows in the Netherlands, Glay and Villemétrie in France, Iona or the lay "colleges" in Great Britain.

---

[4] Mark Gibbs, "For Our Day and Generation," in *Meet the Church,* pp. 31-32.

VI

UNITED STATES AND CANADA: DEFINITION, AWARENESS

In seeking to achieve renewal, the churches of the United States and Canada are not faced with the Europeans' need to discover new channels by which the church may discover the world and the world discover the church. The channels are already operative. Let any newspaper assemble the views of community leaders on any public issue, and among those queried are sure to be spokesmen for the Protestant and Roman Catholic churches. In the United States, church and synagogue membership (voluntary, not automatic as in state churches) reached an all-time high in 1958—sixty-three per cent of the population. At the same time, personal giving to the church and its causes was also setting a new record—$63.27 per member, annually. And in that year a Gallup Poll survey indicated that, in an average week, forty-nine per cent of the adult population attended at least one service in church or synagogue.

In both the United States and Canada, church membership and attendance are socially acceptable, indicating sound standing in the community and, in the former, commitment to the "American way of life." And the laity is anything but lethargic. As nowhere else in the world, North Americans are busy at "church work"—serving on committees, raising funds, sponsoring clubs within the congregation, attending meetings. Growing out of the nineteenth-century concern for expansion of missions, the women's organizations of the major denominations have a history of involvement in money-raising and housekeeping affairs of the local church. Denominationally, they are coordinated on the national level; this centralization has made possible the dissemination of study materials and programs. Most of the denominational men's clubs, coming on the scene later, are likewise coordinated nationally; and through regional and national assemblies their members are spurred to greater activity in the local congregations. Lay leadership training conferences are held at the many denominational summer camps. The National Council of Churches has departments to coordinate these lay activities and encourage joint programs. The NCC women's department, in particular, has spurred creative cooperation in local mission and social action projects. And the council has sponsored nationwide conferences on the nature of the laity's task.

Increasingly, however, concerned people within the American churches, as well as perceptive observers outside their doors, have been asking why, with all this surging lay activity, the effects are not more noticeable. Crime rates continue to climb, the expedient is often the norm in public decisions, materialistic goals alone seem to govern economic and social aspirations, racial tensions flourish, mental breakdowns and family delinquency are common, and a "me first" philosophy widely prevails in both personal and public enterprise.

Perhaps, it is suggested, the trouble lies in laymen's ignorance of what it means to be a Christian, in their faulty conception of what

Christian faith requires of them. Evangelistic crusades that bring people to sign on the dotted line, campaigns that add names to proud church rolls, denominational meetings that glory in attendance records—perhaps all these are futile unless people really act throughout the week as if they were part of Christ's body in the world. There is growing concern because, too often, efforts to stir the laity result simply in more busyness at routine chores of the congregation. Programs of church men's clubs often are designed to please rather than inform or challenge, so that the offering differs little from what the men find in their service club luncheon meetings. And in spite of the imaginative study programs and service projects encouraged by national lay women's organizations, it is probably fair to say that the majority of women in the churches measure the effectiveness of their witness by how successful their money-raising activities prove to be. Nor is it unfair to conclude that most lay men and women look on the church as primarily an institution rather than a body of God's people acting on his behalf in the world. They assume that the clergy, as servants of that institution, are the sole channel through which the Christian ministry is meant to operate, while the laity is liable only for the financial support and housekeeping chores which keep the institution intact and expanding.

Increasingly, concerned and perceptive leaders of the American churches are concluding that the laity lacks not fellowship or action within the congregation so much as an understanding of the Christian faith which will reveal the true nature of the church as a living body in which all are "ministers," witnessing to their faith every day of their lives. While in Europe efforts to bring awareness of such a realization on the part of the laity must be made across a gap of indifference and estrangement, in North America they are to be made within the pews where people sit.

There are signs that many of the people in those pews are coming to be aware of the need for such definition, such realization, in the face of the increasingly strenuous tensions and demands of modern life. Participants in a Methodist conference on Christian education in November, 1959, heard the head of the United States Department of Health, Education, and Welfare declare that spiritual illiteracy is the most serious problem facing the nation today. And a professor from a Methodist seminary told them that signs are multiplying that theirs is a theologically illiterate church. "Our people are beginning to realize that this is so," he said. "Wistful questions keep coming to us: 'Please tell what we believe.'" President Howard Schomer of Chicago Theological Seminary reports the request by a businessman arranging for him to address a church men's club: "Please don't think you have to entertain us. What many of us would like to hear is your understanding of the difference that Christ's coming into the world has really made for mankind; what difference it makes for our own daily struggle at home and at work." In a way, that plea serves to validate the charge that the American churches, by accommodating to their environment instead of confronting and challenging it, are reducing that healthy tension between church and culture that can buttress their own strength and relevance, can prevent the kind of identification with prevailing standards which made the German churches impotent in the Nazi era.

It is impossible in a brief survey to present a picture of all the efforts being made to give American church members opportunity to delve more deeply into the implications of their faith, to reassess the kind of witness they are making to that faith in their daily lives. But a look at certain programs may suggest the variety of approach that is being made. Though some reach beyond the borders of church membership, not many are obliged to find a new way, as are the German academies, to gain the reluctant ear of an estranged world. Rather, they seek to inform and inspire a laity whose members are already committed but unaware of the significance of their commitment.

Communion service "in the round" at Parishfield, Brighton, Michigan

r. H. H. Wolf of Bossey leads discussion of seminary professors at Ecumenical Institute, Evanston, Illinois

Main building of the Austin, Texas, Community's College House

"The House of the Interpreter" at Five Oaks, Paris, Ontario

LOCAL EFFORTS

Perhaps the most typical of such ventures for renewal are those being attempted in local churches, usually by way of courses in basic principles of the Christian faith offered during the week. The Methodist Church's "adult schools of religion" are one example; weekday evening Bible classes in certain local congregations of various denominations are another. At First Presbyterian Church in Rahway, New Jersey, a permanent Laymen's Academy with a full-time dean in charge is devoted to the ministry of the laity. Through ten months of the year the academy offers lecture-seminars on theology, the nature and mission of the church, ethics, and specific problems of home, community, and vocation. In addition, from time to time it sponsors public consultations on lay concerns in cooperation with other churches in the area.

In Evansville, Indiana, and Pittsburgh, Pennsylvania, laymen have responded enthusiastically to invitations to enroll in courses offered, on an interdenominational basis, by the local councils of churches. During the first year of Evansville's "From Discovery to Decision" program, thirteen separate weekday evening and daytime courses—each involving two hours of lecture and discussion weekly, plus extensive reading—ran for two months. Covering four general areas of subject matter (personal growth, Christian horizons, the contemporary search for the meaning of existence in our culture, and the living church), courses dealt with family life, devotional disciplines, Bible study as a background for personal and vocational decisions, the life and thought of Dietrich Bonhoeffer, the Letter to the Ephesians and its implications for God's order today, new insights into the nature of the Christian church, various quests of modern man for the meaning of existence, new methods of evangelism, stewardship, voluntary service in church and community, and skill in human relations. The Pittsburgh experiment has enlisted professors in Pittsburgh-Xenia Theological Seminary to teach courses in theology for laymen, with provision both for beginners and for those ready to undertake more advanced study.

Laymen can delve more deeply into the nature of their faith and church because leaders of certain theological seminaries have decided that their commission to "train young men for the ministry" obliges them to offer training, also, to people engaged in the lay ministry of the church. Thus they answer the appeal of an increasing number of earnest men and women for light on essentials of their faith and insights which may be applied to everyday problems. Officers of the seminaries recognize, too, that such encounters may help keep their own institutions from becoming so ingrown and professionalized that they are islands apart from the ongoing stream of church life.

In the summer of 1959, Lancaster Theological Seminary (Evangelical and Reformed), in Pennsylvania, in cooperation with the men's and women's organizations of the Evangelical and Reformed and the Congregational Christian churches, instituted a Lay School of Theology. It offered two academic courses ("Studies in Pauline Theology" and "Christ, His Church and Our Ministry") and a series of lectures on "Laymen as Counselors" by the chief of Ontario's provincial department of mental health. Within two weeks after announcement of the curriculum, so many had applied for admission that a waiting list had to be instituted. The lay school continued in 1960.

In Berkeley, California, a Laymen's School of Religion, established in the spring of 1959, maintains seminary-level standards in courses for laymen, covering areas of theological thought as related to man's search for understanding, meaning, and purpose in life. Two six-week courses are offered in both fall and spring. In addition, week-end conferences on theological concerns are arranged at frequent intervals. In the fall of 1959, students came from thrity-three different communities within a hundred-mile radius of Berkeley. They represented sixty-seven congregations of eleven denominations. Among them were doctors, dentists, lawyers, architects, engineers, business men and women, housewives, nurses, teachers, university professors, librarians, and directors of religious education in local congregations. Faculty is drawn from the several seminaries in the area: the Church Divinity School of the Pacific (Episcopal), Berkeley Baptist Divinity School, the Pacific School of Religion (interdenominational), San Francisco Theological Seminary (Presbyterian), and Pacific Theological Seminary (Lutheran). Dean of the school is Mrs. Muriel James, an ordained minister. The board of directors is made up of heads of the first four seminaries listed, plus a number of clergymen and laymen from churches in the area. Attracting wide interest, the school is already making a salutary impact on congregational life in the Bay area.

In the fall of 1959, Chicago Theological Seminary (Congregational Christian) established a winterlong course for the laity under the over-all theme "Thinking Theologically About Life's Problems," with enrollment limited to one hundred. Sessions, including lectures by members of the seminary faculty followed by discussion and involving an intensive reading program, were held for two hours on alternate Friday evenings. Theme for the first quarter-term was "Approaches to Christian Belief"; for the second, "Approaches to Christian Action"; for the third, "Christian Approaches to Crucial Social Problems." Sub-themes for study and discussion during the first quarter-term indicate the general direction taken by the course for that period: "The Bible: Myth or Living Word?" "Is the Idea of God Really Dead?" "How Are We to Understand Christ?" "The Holy Spirit and the Spirits of Our Age," and "Misunderstanding of the Church." Admission to the course was on the basis of recommendations sent to the seminary by the applicants' pastors or, in the case of nonchurch members, by educational or religious leaders in the community. In a way, the program is an answer to a suggestion contained in the address given by Howard Schomer when he was inaugurated president of the seminary earlier in the year: "Can a Christian layman possibly make his work as a parent, lawyer, politician, scientist, advertising man, trade-union or industrial leader a veritable witness to the faith if he has never really studied theology? The elaboration of a fresh, dynamic doctrine of the complementary roles of the ordained and nonordained members of the church could give rise to conscious, concerted efforts by lay people, trained and backed by their churches, to make their professional activities actual ministries of the church in the world for which it prays."

Whereas these ventures represent a concern of the church for renewal among laymen already active in its congregations, a program being implemented through the Institute of Christian Social Service at Hartford Theological Seminary, in Connecticut, looks beyond the doors of the church to enter into dialogue with people outside its orbit—a procedure not unlike that of the German academies. It started on its way in the fall of 1959, with a seminar on the social responsibility of mass communications media. In five biweekly sessions, lectures and discussions focused on the ethical implications of the dependence of our economy on the manufacturing of demand as well as of supply, and questioned whether communications media are debasing American culture or fulfilling their avowed purpose of informing the public. Leaders of the separate sessions were experts in the fields being explored: Martin Mayer, author of *Madison Avenue, U.S.A.;* Joseph Bensman, of the William Esty Company; Ernest Dichter, of the Institute for Motivational Research; Gilbert Seldes, of the Annenberg School of Communications; and Harlan Cleveland, of Syracuse University.

EVANSTON ECUMENICAL INSTITUTE

A blending of the two purposes—lay training and church-world encounter—is to be seen in the Evanston (Illinois) Ecumenical Institute which, after four years of intensive planning, was inaugurated in October, 1958. To some extent an outgrowth of local interest aroused by the 1954 meeting in Evanston of the second World Council of Churches Assembly, it represents an imaginative effort to relate the Christian faith to modern problems. An independent venture, it is sponsored by thirteen theological seminaries in the Chicago area. Its affairs are governed by a board made up of representatives of those institutions and leading laymen and clergy. The director, Walter Leibrecht, grew up in Germany, where he was intimately acquainted with the academy movement. He was an exchange student in the United States in 1949-50, returned to Germany to take his doctorate at the University of Heidelberg, then taught at Harvard Divinity School before coming to the Evanston institute. Assisting him in direction of the program is a small permanent staff. In addition, under a grant from a foundation interested in theological education, two scholars took up residence at the center in 1960 to pursue theological research. They are also available for consultation during the conferences and seminars which make up a large part of the institute's program.

The Evanston institute fosters ecumenical contacts and relates the Christian message to modern society (1) by sponsoring scholarly study on contemporary problems, (2) by making it possible for laymen from various denominational backgrounds to explore together the present situation of the churches and their responsibility in that situation, and (3) by sponsoring discussions among members of certain professional and vocational groups. Invitations go directly to members of those groups wherever possible. During its first seven months of operation, the institute was host to thirteen conferences; in addition, its facilities were used by the area's seminaries and university Christian student groups. Some of the regular conferences were concerned with ecumenical issues: Christian missions in the light of the resurgence of indigenous religions in Asia, commitment and tolerance in ecumenical discussion, and early and modern church music, with Protestant, Roman Catholic, and Orthodox theologians interested in liturgical renewal participating. Others brought professional groups to consider common problems: e.g., journalists on "Controversial Issues in a Free Society," businessmen on "Religion and Ethics in Business Decisions." Still others were built around specific themes: "Authority and Love," with psychiatrists, social workers, members of the legal profession, and parents discussing juvenile delinquency; "Atomic Radiation as a Biological and Ethical Problem," with geneticists and physicists debating the implications of recent developments in their fields.

In its second year, the Evanston Ecumenical Institute introduced a winter series of biweekly lectures and discussions open to the general public. Under the direction of Dr. Leibrecht, four sessions were devoted to presentations of the thought of Albert Schweitzer, Karl Barth, Reinhold Niebuhr, and Paul Tillich; four to a survey of the careers and specific contributions of pioneers in the ecumenical movement; four to developing an understanding of the Christian faith. Meanwhile, a comprehensive program of one- and two-day conferences and seminars was attracting increasing interest in the community, and news of the venture began to find its way into the metropolitan press. There were meetings for businessmen, for people leaving to work in branches of American industry overseas, for social workers, for scientists, for physicians. There were consultations on religion in industry, on religion and the public schools, on the challenge of modern art to the churches, on the responsibility of the laity, on the role of the family in contemporary society, on the relation between church and world, and on the institute itself. There were frequent seminars on aspects of church unity, worldwide and local.

Now housed in a spacious old residence with upstairs auditorium, on a tree-shaded street a few doors from its original rented quarters, the Evanston Ecumenical Institute can offer some lodging for participants who come from a distance. The house has a growing library, comfortable conference and social rooms, facilities for dining. As the program expands, the staff hopes to do a bit of "extension" work, helping congregations in the area conduct workshops on regular conference themes, making use of resources and findings developed during the sessions. Already it has been demonstrated that the conferences have a way of growing beyond themselves. After seventy-five Chicago-area women had attended a spring conference at the institute on "The Nature of Ecumenical

Understanding," they requested more light on the subject; in response, the staff arranged a series of five study sessions for further exploration.

'FAITH AND LIFE' INSTITUTES

A similar dual aim—lay training and encounter with the problems of the modern world—lies at the heart of a creative venture in the United Lutheran Church in America. At its 1956 convention, it asked the Board of Social Missions to explore the possibility of establishing a program of discussion and fellowship that would achieve, in North America, results similar to those of the Evangelical academies in Germany. Recognizing that churches in North America and Germany operate in different milieux, the board determined that such a program should (1) interpret the Christian faith to the laity and (2) relate that faith to vocational and civic life. It saw as the gap to be bridged not so much one of antagonism between church and world as one of irrelevance splitting the professed faith of the laity from the responsibilities borne by the laity in daily life.

The committee charged with getting the new program under way realized at once that it would be wasting energy if it tried to reach *all* the laity with a campaign type of approach. So it decided to work with small groups, in which intensive discussion and analysis could take place among people holding special responsibilities in church and society. As a pilot experiment, it conducted five "Faith and Life Institutes" between September, 1957, and March, 1958. At Elim Lodge, in Ontario, eighty-two "average laymen" and five pastors met to discuss "The Outreach of the Christian Life," using the denomination's *Christian Social Responsibility* (a three-volume study course) as resource material. In Des Moines, Iowa, thirty-six farmers and nine pastors explored "The Farmer Under the Impact of Technology." At Santa Barbara, California, twenty-four representatives of middle and upper levels of business management discussed ethical implications in the "organization man" phenomenon. Results indicated that the men hesitated to recognize that ethical implications were involved. At Washington, D. C., seventy-two people considered the changing role of women in public life. To a greater degree than elsewhere, frank self-searching characterized the final institute, held at Columbia University's Arden House, near Harriman, New York, where thirteen physicians, a nurse, and five clergymen discussed "The Science of Man and the Practice of Medicine."

The preparations for each of the pilot institutes were made by a regional committee including representatives of the vocation to be viewed. In each case, the three-day session began with Bible study and basic lectures on the theme, followed by group discussion. From the difficulty participants had relating theological perspective to concrete life situations, leaders recognized a deep need for more such joint exploration. Since attendance had been solicited through pastors' offices, participation was confined almost entirely to United Lutherans active in their own congregations. Here was the church's own laity, itself a part of the "world," whose values and standards cried out to be brought under the scrutiny of Christian principle.

On the basis of the six-month pilot experimenting, the United Lutheran Church commissioned the board to develop the program further, and a staff member was called to give full time to its direction. As it has proceeded, the program has settled into a two-pronged pattern: (1) denomination-wide study and discussion by pastors and laymen of Christian social responsibility, against a background of theological exposition; (2) extension of the two- or three-day Faith and Life Institutes throughout the United States and Canada. The vocational institutes will be introduced through men's and women's organizations, then implemented in smaller conferences to reach laymen not yet active in congregational life. It is hoped that, as men and women in the pews thus discover their Christian responsibility in everyday actions and decisions, renewal will be a force growing out of the congregation itself, not penetrating from the outside as it necessarily must in Germany.

PARISH LIFE PROGRAM

Renewal within the parish is also the aim of a pilot experiment the Protestant Episcopal Church has been conducting for the past seven years. Its Parish Life Program is designed to take parish "busyness"— raising funds, holding meetings, promoting fellowship—out of the realm of the casual and the taken for granted by providing the average layman with a reason for his activity, enabling him to speak about what the church is, and giving him a Christian motivation in all aspects of his daily life.

The Parish Life Program makes its initial entry into the life of the congregation when a group of lay men and women, only some of whom are already in posts of parish leadership, attend a weekend conference along with about thirty people from as many as six other parishes. In exploratory discussion, the participants subject what goes on in their home parishes to critical study; to many of them, the question of why they raise money, conduct bazaars, or go to meetings has never before occurred. Then, in a second approach, the conferees consider the deepest needs of people in today's world. Actual case studies are presented involving Episcopalians who have faced critical personal problems and found no solutions. In the light of the previous discussion about home parish activities, the laymen consider what help their own parishes could have offered these people. By the time the week end is over, the laymen, with the help of trained leaders prepared to offer theological insights, have made acquaintance with such terms as sin, guilt, salvation, redemption, acceptance, and rejection, and have faced up to searching self-analysis, viewing what goes on—and doesn't go on—in their home parishes from a new perspective. Leaders are careful to avoid pat answers or suggest specific techniques when the inevitable query "What can *we* do?" comes. The value of the conferences lies not in having answers supplied, but in recognizing needs, becoming aware of what the church really is and what responsibility being a member entails. Parish renewal will come, leaders of the program believe, when individuals and the parish begin to "live out" the answers to such questions as "How can we more effectively carry out our ministry as church members?" "How can we carry our vision of our Christian responsibility into the daily round of our lives?" and "How can our parish become a truly redemptive community?"

Originally directed by the Protestant Episcopal Church's national department of Christian education, the Parish Life conferences are now the responsibility of diocesan Christian education departments. Along with the broader conferences, Parish Life missions have been developed in local communities. Here parish lay leaders and potential leaders meet nightly for a week to analyze man's fundamental predicaments, discuss the essentials of the Christian faith, then consider what continuing application of new insights can be made in congregational life. The entire Parish Life program has proved salutary on an experimental basis; eventually, it may be introduced on a wider scale throughout the denomination.

CLARENDON HILLS

At a lay center housed in buildings on a newly acquired farm in Clarendon Hills, north of Toronto, the Presbyterian Church in Canada is implementing the program which the denomination commissioned by establishing an interboard Committee on the Laity and appointing a secretary to coordinate congregational efforts to make more vital the role of laymen in their church and in their daily work. The venture is still in the experimental stage, with concrete plans to be evolved as events and research reveal the greatest needs. Meanwhile, one project is already under way. At the Clarendon Hills center, a program of week-end retreats brings together local lay men and women eager to learn more about Christian witness in daily living, people who perhaps have long pondered questions about the faith they profess on Sundays but have not voiced them for fear of being squelched with arbitrary and unilluminating answers. Together with a few clergymen, they share the community life of the farm, discuss basic questions of life and work, and participate in joint exploration of Bible passages and in meditation growing out of the discussions. Thus they strive to grasp the meaning of the Word of God not, as a statement from the center's leadership puts it, that they may be "more knowledgeable on Sundays," but that they may be "the truly living persons they want to be every day of their lives." Canadian Presbyterian leaders hope that such retreats, along with more extensive future conferences, will produce a responsible congregational leadership.

FIVE OAKS

Operating on a more independent basis than Clarendon Hills, but still maintaining a definite denominational relationship, is another lay institution in Ontario. Near Paris, high on a bluff overlooking Grand River, stands the Five Oaks Christian Workers Center, so named because it receives part of its financial support from the five central conferences of the United Church of Canada. The spreading, two-story, split-level "House of the Interpreter" has accommodations for eighty-five guests and a ten-member staff, besides space for three large assembly halls, several classrooms, a library, and a chapel. At the foot of the bluff, two lodges and fourteen cabins designed for summer conferences and camps can house an additional one hundred twenty-five people in emergencies.

Operating autonomously under its own board, Five Oaks exists "to help lay people learn to make a clear Christian witness in their work, their homes, and their church." The program is four-pronged: (1) Five month-long conferences are offered (in January, February, March, July, and August) at which laymen who would like to become more adequate church members study principles of the Christian faith, the Bible, church history, Christian understanding of personality, and techniques of Christian education. The study is carried on through the media of research projects, reading, panel discussions, and instruction by members of the staff. Considerable attention is given to the art of Christian communication. Thus far, laymen from a wide variety of professions—physicians, housewives, secretaries, nurses, teachers, farmers, manual and office workers—have taken part in the intensive four-week courses. (2) Week-end conferences are held throughout the year for people working within a specific profession. They discuss their occupational problems under the theme "The Layman and His Daily Work." These conferences are promoted, and the invitations extended, not through the churches but through the vocational group concerned. So far, the most successful of the week-end meetings have been those attended by nurses, teachers, and farmers. In fact, the staff is convinced that the discussions at Five Oaks have exerted a salutary influence on the region's agricultural affairs and on the content of training courses for nurses. (3) Ten annual retreats offer laymen an opportunity for meditation—"quiet listening to God." Skilled, specially-trained retreat leaders are on hand to share their insights with the men and women who participate. (4) A summer program has three facets: weeklong training conferences for workers in Christian education, family and youth camps, and a vocational guidance course. In addition, the center's facilities are available during the Christmas and Easter holidays to teen-agers who confer on their special interests and concerns.

Though associated with the church, Five Oaks is entirely autonomous and people of all denominations are welcome to share in its programs. (This open-door policy, prevails, incidentally, at all the lay centers so far established in North America, no matter under what auspices they operate or what their denominational background.) Also related to the United Church of Canada are three smaller lay centers: at Fort Qu'Appelle, Saskatchewan; at Tatamagouche, Nova Scotia; and at Naramata, British Columbia. Though they differ in program details and in emphasis, they share a single purpose—to help laymen make more effective Christian witness in their daily work and in the lives of their congregations.

In a number of centers in the United States efforts are being made to help the laity of the churches become something more than a passive audience for the preacher on Sunday morning. When possible, they bring that laity an awareness not only of the pertinence of the Christian faith to issues of the present day, but also an understanding of those issues so that theological insights may have vital relevance to the modern world.

PENDLE HILL

Oldest of these centers is Pendle Hill, established by Quakers at Wallingford, near Philadelphia, in 1930. There a program of lectures, study, discussion, and meditation is designed to lead to development of a relevant religious insight. Each year students enroll for three eleven-week courses, or for one three-week course involving full-time study. In addition, frequent week-end conferences, seminars, and retreats deal intensively with specific questions. In line with Pendle Hill's watchword, borrowed from William Penn—"True godliness does not turn men out of the world but enables them to live better in it and excites their endeavors to mend it"—social studies are directed toward the need for reconciliation in industrial, racial, and international relations. Regularly, labor institutes train men for union responsibilities and, on occasion, bring representatives of labor and management together for joint conferences. Frequent seminars and discussion meetings relate the gospel to various aspects of modern culture. Physical labor, "Quaker silence," recreation, and creative arts have their places on the schedule. Out of the extensive study and research carried on at the center have come a remarkable series of Pendle Hill pamphlets which have met eager acceptance in and beyond Quaker circles. People from all denominations—and from none—and from all walks of life are to be found participating in the Pendle Hill community; some pursue the formal courses of study, others carry on independent research.

PARISHFIELD

In 1948, the Protestant Episcopal diocese of Michigan established a residential center at Parishfield, a farm near Brighton, Michigan. The diocese grants use of the property (on which are now a main house, dormitory and dining facilities for thirty-two guests, staff houses, and a library-chapel building) to the Parishfield community and contributes to its support, but the program is entirely autonomous. Members of the staff, their families, and the guests make up a compact worshiping, working, and studying group. Consciously ecumenical, Parishfield welcomes clergy and laity from all confessions to its continuing series of conferences. Conferees are challenged by the presentation of the Christian faith as something more than successful-on-the-surface "religion in general."

The Parishfield staff, which arranges the conferences and coordinates findings for further study and discussion, is convinced that unless laymen discover in Christianity something more than a prop for the "American way of life," that way becomes the religion of the churches themselves. The discussions, aimed against such a threat, encourage blunt questions about the nation's touted "religious revival," and honest search to discover what the nature of the church really is. Lay people are led to realize that they are the essence of the church, the instrument through which God's redeeming work is to be done in the world. The Parishfield program makes room for meaningful worship, but it encourages no withdrawal, no passive waiting. It aims to prod, to awaken.

An example of the outreach of Parishfield is its involvement with the work of the Detroit Industrial Mission, an imaginative experiment initiated in 1956 by Episcopal parishes in Detroit to discover the role of the church in a completely industrialized society. Full-time workers on the mission staff go "where people are" to learn how the Christian faith rates with men whose working hours are spent in the great automobile factories. Then, at week-end conferences at Parishfield—an hour's ride from the outskirts of Detroit—

groups of the men who have been contacted meet to consider basic problems of the assembly line in relation to the Christian faith. One such group debated whether Christianity is concerned at all about what is going on in the world; another, made up of union leaders, considered whether domestic or international budgets should be given priority in the economizing efforts of the union. The staff of the mission, which is now out of the pilot stage, maintains a continuous, unobtrusive relationship with men and women at their places of work—in factories, offices, union halls, trade association headquarters—on both an individual and a group basis. It cooperates with clergy and laity in four established Episcopal parishes in Detroit in a discussion and study program designed to make the content of sermon and liturgy come alive in everyday activity, and it carries its work to parish and diocesan groups throughout Michigan and elsewhere.

In America today the major Protestant churches, particularly in the larger urban areas, do not enlist large numbers of factory workers. However, as concern develops to make the church serve all people, certain conscious efforts—of which the Detroit mission is one—are being made to extend the church's ministry beyond its doors without the inhibiting aim of "adding new members." Scattered experiments of this nature throughout the nation's Episcopal constituency are coordinated by a special department of the denomination's national council.

PACKARD MANSE

While the facilities of Packard Manse, the lay study and retreat center at Stoughton, Massachusetts, are most frequently used by students and faculty of the colleges and universties in the area, it is host from time to time to groups of laymen interested in relating their faith to "the world." For the center's purpose is to encourage dialogue between church and world, to the benefit of each. Interdenominational in practice and sponsorship, it is operated by an independent agency, the Christian Fellowship Foundation. On the board of trustees are professors from Boston area universities and technical institutes, businessmen, housewives, artists—representing at least a half-dozen different denominations. On the conference program have been vocational consultations (for teachers, accountants, politicians, architects, lawyers), as well as discusions of specific problems in public life. In the fall of 1959, the center cooperated with the American Baptist Home Mission Society's division of evangelism in bringing together people of the area in a series of four pilot conferences on the responsibility of the layman in his vocation. Each consultation in the series assembled people with common responsibilities in some particular area. For instance, in late October a group of people connected nonprofessionally with the public schools—school board members, P.T.A. workers, and so on—looked at such issues as budgets, bond issues, parent-teacher relationships, attacks on the public school system, and parochial education.

The program at Packard Manse remains flexible. As Director Paul Chapman points out, "We have found that Packard Manse means different things to different people, depending on their perspective. There has been a deliberate effort to keep doors open for continued development in several areas for, unlike the parish, there is little modern precedent for the church centers. It is still not clear what path will be the most significant one to follow." But like the leaders of the other centers, Mr. Chapman is sure of the need for such experimenting: "There are times when new depths can be discovered in new structures, for the old structures tend to degenerate into rules and regulations. The walls that separate the church in our society from the world are sometimes tragically high, and the fact that Jesus Christ came into the world to eliminate the divisions which exist between the priestly class and those who would find religious significance in the daily round is often forgotten. Too frequently, the truth of the gospel is isolated within the temple, with little chance for the redemption of man in Christ to mean anything in the ambiguous lives we all must live in home, work, and recreation. To fulfill its task the church must enter into a dialogue with the world; it must mature in its understanding of itself and its role in the world. No one can speak with authority who does not know the realistic problems of making decisions in today's culture. The life of a center for lay renewal is involved with revitalization of the significance of the *kerygma* in the context of our complex culture."

There are, in the United States, a number of movements whose purpose is to strengthen the adherents' commitment to the Christian faith by individual and group spiritual disciplines and exercises. Some among them are esoteric and withdrawn, concentrating only on their members' personal concerns. But others encourage such discipline as a foundation for involvement with concerns of "the world," seeking consciously to translate commitment into action.

KIRKRIDGE

Kirkridge, a rural mountainside center near Bangor, in eastern Pennsylvania, combines opportunity for fellowship among a group of clergy and laity who keep a disciplined spiritual rule of life (the "Kirkridge Discipline") with a program of retreats and conferences at which people of all denominations and walks of life are welcome. It is the focus for a "movement for power among the churches," initiated in 1942 by a group of churchmen concerned to enable people from various races and creeds to deepen their faith by worship, quiet, exchange of ideas, and hard work; to discover their unity with like-minded Christians; and to consider taking action at those points where the Christian faith confronts modern culture. The discipline by which the inner circle of the community is bound calls for daily prayer (for which a lectionary is provided), identification with the suffering of others, practice of nonviolence, assumption of responsibility in local congregations, cooperation in the wider Christian fellowship, and stewardship of time, energy, and money. It calls also for participation with others in a "nurture group" and attendance at retreats.

This nucleus of men and women keeps the Kirkridge Discipline and reports on it quarterly, while thousands of others have taken part in the conferences and retreats. These programs are designed to further the aims of the movement, to contribute to the building up of an informed laity, and to provide fellowship in physical work, Bible study, worship, and recreation. Through a typical season (late April to the end of October) groups of people may be found at separate conferences on topics ranging from spiritual healing, through the problems of the inner city, to "renewal of the inner life." Some conferences are on an invitational basis. Some are designed for particular groups; e.g., mothers of young children, seminary students, alcoholics. Throughout, the emphasis obviously is less on fostering encounter between church and world than on encouraging deeper and more active commitment on the part of the already committed. Both emphases have a part in renewal.

OTHER MOVEMENTS

A somewhat similar joining of ventures involving dedication to a disciplined rule of devotional life with meetings for discussion, discovery, and renewal is represented by the Yokefellow Movement, which centers in Yokefellow House near Earlham College (Quaker), in Richmond, Indiana, where Elton Trueblood, who inspired creation of the movement, is a member of the faculty. The movement operates through circles of active laymen of various denominations who practice a daily regimen of prayer and Bible reading, and meet across denominational and parish lines in "cells" to "listen to the spirit" and gain new strength and perspectives for the challenges of daily living. To Yokefellow House for week-end retreats come groups from churches far and near. In addition, occasional institutes featuring lectures and discussions are offered for members of specific occupational groups. For instance, in the fall of 1959 separate conferences brought to the house coaches and athletic directors, college administrators and faculty members, labor union personnel, high school teachers and administrators, and retired and preparing-to-retire men and women.

Dedicated to the proposition that the problems of individuals and of society are basically spiritual, an organization known as the Laymen's Movement for a Christian World has since 1941 conducted research projects and sponsored seminars and retreats at its headquarters, Wainwright House, a mansion on an estate near Rye, New York. Operating on an international, non-sectarian basis, the movement concentrates on making it possible for small groups of church members, active in the business and professional world, to explore the nature of their spiritual and social responsibilities. Leadership of the seminars and retreats is drawn from top professional and business circles. For some years research and subject matter at retreats was devoted pretty much to spiritual healing. Today, however, the main emphasis is on strengthening businessmen who undertake to apply their Christian faith to the day-to-day decisions in their work. The movement has sponsored a number of seminars on "Spiritual Foundations of Business Practice," not only at Wainwright House but in various cities around the country. The headquarters staff assists in the building up of "cells" of businessmen who meet regularly to pray together and discuss common problems and spiritual concerns. There are now about fifty such cells in twenty cities. On the international level the movement has enrolled people in forty-five countries in a pledge to support world political leaders with prayer. And it has promoted international visits among people who share similar spiritual concerns. It led in the successful campaign to have a meditation room established in the United Nations headquarters building, and in the effort to have a prayer room set aside aside in the United States capitol. Until 1957, it sponsored the annual observance of Laymen's Sunday, now a project of the National Council of Churches' Department of United Church Men. Though actual membership in the movement is under two thousand (with most in the United States and Canada and a few in fourteen other countries), it exerts quite a bit of influence because so many members are prominent in their vocations. The United Nations recognizes it as a nongovernmental organization, and it is represented at sessions of that body in New York by an official observer.

Aims similar to those of the Laymen's Movement inform the program of Shadybrook House, a lay center established in 1957 in a residence leased from the Holden Arboretum, near Cleveland, by a group of men who had been active in the Wainwright House retreats and sought to provide a focus for the movement in Ohio. Still operating on a small, somewhat experimental scale, it offers one- and two-day retreats and seminars on aspects of spiritual growth. Its facilities are frequently used by groups from churches in the area.

AUSTIN COMMUNITY

Quite unlike any one of the ventures described above, yet incorporating certain features of all on a most comprehensive scale, is the Christian Faith-and-Life Community in Austin, Texas. Interdenominational and interracial, governed by a board made up of Austin area ministers and laymen representing various professions, it experiments frankly to discover how theological education for the layman may be developed most effectively. In its University branch some ninety men and women students from the nearby University of Texas live in two houses a block apart, share common meals, worship together daily in the community chapel, and participate in a ten-hours-weekly program (over and above their regular class schedule) which offers lectures, seminars, and discussion on theology, the nature and history of the church, and the relation of the church to the modern world. A similar program is carried on for married students who live in apartments in the neighborhood. Twice monthly, "alumni" of the study course have the privilege of returning for a week end of further study, and discussion of their experience as laymen "out in the world."

The "alumni" phase of the program is one of the wide variety of activities offered by the Christian Faith-and-Life Community at its Laos branch, which occupies a spacious mansion several blocks from the university center. There a continuous series of residential conferences and courses and week-end retreats is attended by groups of clergy and laymen from churches throughout south-central Texas. In lectures, seminars, study sessions, and discussions, people from all walks of life and all age groups confront the implications of the gospel and their bearing on modern dilemmas. In 1959, the community initiated a formal series of basic theological studies for laymen under the direction of the seven theologians on its staff. Offering both beginning and advanced studies, the series is designed particularly for people anxious to discover meaning in human existence from the Christian perspective. In still another emphasis, seminars directed by practitioners of the various arts provide an objective "dialogue with culture." For men and women in the Austin area, the study courses are conducted on Thursday evenings through three annual six-week terms; for those who live elsewhere in the region the same material is presented on scheduled week ends during which the participants live at Laos House. Word of the experiment at Austin has spread, and in other university communities adaptations of the plan to provide serious theological training alongside regular studies in other academic disciplines are being considered. Since the work is "extra," only unusually able and dedicated students are encouraged to undertake it.

After an initial meeting of directors of lay centers in the United States and Canada in 1958, annual gatherings for exchange of ideas and experiences have been held. But no permanent central organization has emerged—which perhaps is just as well. Spontaneous in origin and varied in approach, these pioneer ventures are handicapped by neither tradition nor "approved" regulations. They operate in a milieu far different from that which surrounds the lay centers in continental Europe but, like them, they represent—each in its own way—a reflection of the growing concern throughout Protestantism that the church should gain an awareness of the real nature of the problems and perplexities besetting the world, and seek—through her laity—to bring to bear an informed witness on those issues.

Constituting a clearing house for information on ways in which the laity the world over is seeking to fulfill its role, as well as a source of study material on the nature of that role, is the World Council of Churches' Department on the Laity, with headquarters in Geneva. Pertinent to its labors, as to the work of all the ventures on behalf of the laity, is a paragraph from the report adopted by the World Council's 1954 Assembly: "The real battles of faith today are being fought in factories, shops, offices and farms, in political parties and government agencies, in countless homes, in the press, radio and television, in the relationship of nations. Very often it is said that the Church should 'go into' these spheres, but the fact is that the Church already *is* in these spheres in the person of its laity."

None of the lay centers, in Europe or North America, claims to be more than an experiment involving a few of many laymen; none proposes to replace the traditional pattern of parish life, but all hope to reinforce and renew that life. They were founded by concerned Christians who see the "secular" world as peopled by men and women who are God's children; because this is so they seek not to conquer but to serve. And in all of them, as in any venture imaginatively, honestly, and unselfishly conducted, there is a nucleus of hope for the future.

A DIRECTORY OF LAY CENTERS AND MOVEMENTS IN EUROPE AND NORTH AMERICA

FINLAND

Lay Centers:

Lärkulla-Stiftelsen, Kaaris. Director: Harry Eugen Georg Wentzel.

Suomen Kirken Sourakunta Opisto, Järvenpää, Tuusula. Director: Simo Palosuo.

FRANCE

Lay Centers:

Centre de Glay, Doubs, Montbéliard. Director: J. Lochard.

Centre de Liebfrouenberg, Strasbourg.

Centre de Recontre Cormatin, Cormatin (Saône et Loire).

Centre de Villemétrie, Villemétrie par Senlis (Oisê). Director: A. de Robert.

Centre Régional Protestant, Petit Château du Lac, Le Nouvion-en-Thiérache (Aisne). Director: G. Richard-Molard.

Protestant Religious Community:

Taizé Communauté, Cormatin (Saône et Loire). Prior: Roger Schütz.

GERMANY

Evangelical Academies:

Baden (Herrenalb): Blumenstrasse 1, Karlsruhe. Director: Hans Schomerus.

Bavaria: Schloss Tutzing, am Starnberger See. Directors: Gerhard Hildmann, Adolf Sommerauer.

Berlin: Jebensstrasse 1, Berlin-Charlottenburg 2. Directors: Dr. Erich Müller-Gangloff, Dr. Alfred Schmidt.

Hamburg: Esplanade 16, Hamburg 36. Director: Gerhard Günther.

Hannover: Loccum über Wunstorf. Directors: Johannes Doehring, Dr. Hans Bolewski.

Hessen-Nassau (Arnoldshain): bei Schmitten/Taunus. Schaumainkai 23, Frankfurt/M. Directors: Dr. Hans Kallenbach, Dr. Heinrich Renkewitz.

Kurhessen-Waldeck: Schlösschen Schönburg, Hofgeismar. Directors: Dr. Werner Jentsch, Dr. Hermann Noack.

Mecklenburg (East Zone): Güstrow/Dom, Güstrow. Director: Gerhard Bosinski.

Mülheim (Haus der Begegnung): Uhlenhorstweg 29, Mülheim/Ruhr, Westphalia. Director: Karl Krämer.

Oldenburg: Amalienstrasse 6, Oldenburg i. O. Director: Dr. Schultz.

Pfalz (Palatinate): Domplatz 2. Speyer/Rhein. Weinstrasse Süd 87, Bad Dürkheim. Director: K. Köhler.

Rheinland-Westphalia: Haus Ortlohn, Baarstrasse 59, Hemer, Kreis Iserlohn/Westphalia. Director: Wilhelm Becker.

Saxony (East Zone): Jüdenberg 17, Meissen/Elbe. Director: Georg Muntschick.

Saxony-Anhalt (East Zone): am Dom 2, Magdeburg. Director: Dr. Lothar Kreyssig.

Schleswig-Holstein: Friedrichstrasse 75, Schleswig. Director: Friedrich Heyer.

Sozialakademie Friedewald: Friedewald über Betzdorf/Sieg. Directors: Dr. Gerhard Heilfurth, Dr. E. Thier.

Thüringen (East Zone): am Steinborn 33, Jena. Director: H. Waldmann.

Württemberg: Bad Boll über Göppingen, Württemberg. Directors: Dr. Eberhard Müller, Hans Stroh.

Church-Industry Projects:

Haus Villigst, Schwerte (Ruhr), Westphalia.

Gossner Mission, Gen. Mudra Strasse 1-3, Mainz-Kastel, Hessen.

Kirchentag:

Deutscher Evangelischer Kirchentag, Magdeburger Strasse 19, Fulda, Hessen.

GREAT BRITAIN

Iona Community: Isle of Iona, via Oban, Scotland. (Winter, Candlemakers' Hall, Candlemakers' Row, Edinburgh 1, Scotland.) Directors: George F. MacLeod, T. Ralph Morton.

Iona Community House: 214 Clyde Street, Glasgow C.1, Scotland. Warden: J. Maitland.

Training Colleges:

Moor Park College, Farnham, Surrey, England. Warden: Canon R. E. Parsons.

William Temple College, Rugby, Warwickshire, England. Warden: Canon L. Hodgson.

Y.M.C.A. Colleges (Cheshunt, Coleg y Fro, Dunford, Kingsgate, St. Cuthbert's): National Council of Y.M.C.A.'s, 112, Great Russell Street, London, W.C.1, England.

INTERNATIONAL

Castle Mainau (Y.M.C.A.), Insel Mainau (Bodensee), Germany.

The Directors' Association of the Laymen's Colleges in Europe, Bad Boll über Göppingen, Württemberg, Germany. Director: Horst Birk.

Ecumenical Institute, Château de Bossey, Bossey/Céligny, Switzerland. Director: H. H. Wolf.

Friends International Center (Clarens, Switzerland): American Friends Service Committee, 20 S. 12th Street, Philadelphia, U. S. A.

ITALY

Ecumenical Community and Retreat Center:

Agape, Praly-di-Perrero, Torino. Director: Tullio Vinay.

THE NETHERLANDS

Lay Training and Conference Centers:

Den Alerdinck: Heino, Laag Zuthem. Leader: K. van Drimmelen.

Arbeidersgemeenschap der Woodbrookers: Bentveld and Kortehemmen, Bentveldweg 3. Directors: Dr. A. van Biemen, W. H. Buys.

De Breede: No. 16 te Breede (Post Warffum). Leader: P. A. Geluk.

De Haaf:Natteweg 9, Bergen (N.H.). Leaders: M. J. Groeneveld, M. Voors.

Hedenesse: O. 8 te Cadzand (Zws. Vlaanderen). Leader: R. J. Wasterval.

Kerk en Wereld Institute: Hoofdstraat 211, Driebergen. Directors of Conference Work: Dr. J. M. van Veen, G. van den Akker, C. I. Dales, W. Vogel.

Oud Poelgeest: Oegstgeest. Leaders: A. W. Kist, C. M. Baronesse van Heemstra, J. M. Hoekstra.

SWEDEN

Lay Foundations:

Geijer School: Ransäter. Director: Ingvar Sahlin.
Hjälmseryd Foundation: Stockaryd. Director: Ingvar Hector.
Sigtuna Foundation: Sigtuna. Director: Olov Hartman.
St. Katherine's Foundation: Sparreholms Slott, Sparreholm. Director: Dr. Margit Sahlin.

SWITZERLAND

Heimstätte:

Boldern: Männedorf, Kanton Zurich. Director: Dr. H. J. Rinderknecht.
Crêt-Bérard: par Puidoux, Vaud. Director: Ch. Nicole-Debarge.
Haus Rüdlingen: Pfarrweg 1, Schaffhausen. Director: R. Sigg.
Seengen: Aargau. Director: K. Naef.
Vaumarcus: Vaumarcus, Neuchâtel. Director: G. Roulet, Bevaix.

UNITED STATES AND CANADA

Lay Training Centers:

Clarendon Hills: Presbyterian Church in Canada, Board of Christian Education, 63 St. George Street, Toronto 5, Ontario, Canada. Secretary for Lay Studies: S. B. Coles.
Christian Faith-and-Life Community, 2503 Rio Grande, Austin 5, Texas. Director: W. Jack Lewis.
Evanston Ecumenical Institute, Ridge and Grove Avenues, Evanston, Illinois. Director: Walter Leibrecht.
Five Oaks Christian Workers Center, Paris, Ontario, Canada. Directors: B. L. Oaten, Jane Bone.
Kirkridge: Bangor, Pennsylvania. Resident Director: Joseph E. Platt.
Packard Manse: 583 Plain Street, Stoughton, Massachusetts. Resident Director: Paul K. Chapman.
Parishfield: Brighton, Michigan. Director: Francis Ayres.
Pendle Hill: 383 Plush Mill Road, Wallingford, Pennsylvania. Resident Director: Dan Wilson.
Shadybrook House: R.F.D. No. 1, Mentor, Ohio. Director: Donald R. Boyce.
Wainwright House (Laymen's Movement for a Christian World): Milton Point, Rye, New York. Secretary: Wayman C. Huckabee.
Yokefellow House (Yokefellow Movement): 228 College Avenue, Richmond, Indiana. Director: Samuel Emerick.

Other Lay Enterprises:

Detroit Industrial Mission: 24699 Grand River Avenue, Detroit 19, Michigan. Director: Hugh C. White, Jr.

Chicago Theological Seminary Course for Laymen: 5751 South Woodlawn Avenue, Chicago, Illinois. Administrative Director: C. V. Giddings.

Evansville Faith and Life Institute: Evansville Council of Churches, 203 YMCA Building, Evansville, Indiana.

Hartford Seminary Foundation Institute of Church and Community: 55 Elizabeth Street, Hartford, Connecticut. Director: Peter L. Berger.

Lay School of Theology, Lancaster Theological Seminary, Lancaster, Pennsylvania.

Laymen's School of Religion, P. O. Box 655, Berkeley 1, California. Dean: Mrs. Muriel James.

National Council of Churches Departments of United Church Men and United Church Women: 475 Riverside Drive, New York 27, New York.

Pittsburgh Courses for Laymen: Council of Churches of the Pittsburgh Area, 220 Grant Street, Pittsburgh 19, Pennsylvania.

Protestant Episcopal Parish Life Program: National Council Department of Christian Education, 28 Havemeyer Street, Greenwich, Connecticut. Director: Sumner Walters, Jr.

Rahway Laymen's Academy: West Grand Avenue and Church Street, Rahway, New Jersey. Dean: W. H. Cohea, Jr.

United Lutheran Faith and Life Institutes: 231 Madison Avenue, New York 6, New York. Director: Rufus Cornelson.

A READING LIST

Bonhoeffer, Dietrich. *The Cost of Discipleship.* Translated by R. H. Fuller. London: Student Christian Movement Press, 1948; revised and enlarged edition, New York: Macmillan, 1959.

———. *Ethics.* Edited by Eberhard Bethge. Translated by W. H. Smith. New York: Macmillan, 1955.

Calhoun, Robert L. *God and the Day's Work.* New York: Association (Reflection Books), 1957.

Congar, Yves M. J. *Lay People in the Church.* Translated by Donald Altwater. Westminster, Md.: Newman, 1957.

Dietrich, Suzanne de. *The Witnessing Community.* Philadelphia: Westminster, 1958.

Kraemer, Hendrik. *A Theology of the Laity.* Philadelphia: Westminster, 1958.

*MacLeod, George F. *Only One Way Left.* Glasgow: Iona Community, 1956.

Miller, Alexander. *Christian Faith and My Job.* New York: Association (Reflection Books), 1959.

*Morton, T. Ralph. *The Household of Faith.* Glasgow: Iona Community, 1951.

———. *The Community of Faith.* U. S. edition with added chapters by Alexander Miller and John Oliver Nelson. New York: Association, 1954.

Nelson, John Oliver, ed. *Work and Vocation.* New York: Harper, 1954.

Newbigin, J. E. Lesslie. *The Household of God.* New York: Friendship, 1954.

Niebuhr, H. Richard, and others. *The Purpose of the Church and Its Ministry.* New York: Harper, 1956.

Oldham, J. H. *Life Is Commitment.* New York: Association (Reflection Books), 1959.

Southcott, Ernest W. *The Parish Comes Alive.* New York: Morehouse-Gorham, 1956.

Visser 't Hooft, W. A. *The Renewal of the Church.* Philadelphia: Westminster, 1957.

Ward, Leo R. *Catholic Life, U. S. A.: Contemporary Lay Movements.* New York: Herder, 1959.

Weber, Hans-Ruedi, ed. *Meet the Church* (the Kirchentag movement). Geneva: The World Council of Churches Department on the Laity, 1959.

———. *Signs of Renewal* (the lay centers in Europe). Geneva: The World Council of Churches Department on the Laity, 1956. Revised 1957.

———. *A Symposium on the Laity* (articles reprinted from the *Ecumenical Review,* Vol. X, No. 3, April 1958). Geneva: World Council of Churches Department on the Laity, 1958.

Wickham, E. R. *Church and People in an Industrial City.* New York: Hillary, 1958.

Wingren, Gustav. *Luther on Vocation.* Philadelphia: Muhlenberg, 1957.

*Winslow, Jack C. *The Lee Abbey Story.* London: Lutterworth, 1956.

---

* British titles available from Alec Allenson, Naperville, Illinois.

INDEX